## Minnesota & Western Wisconsin Trails

### Where to Go · What to Expect · How to Get There

*By Marlys & Phil Mickelson*

Second Printing
All rights reserved.
Adventure Publications, Inc.
PO Box 269
Cambridge, Minnesota 55008

Copyright 1999
ISBN 1-885061-20-X
Front cover photo: Bill Marchel

Printed in Canada

## Dedication:

This book is dedicated to a diverse group of energetic individuals whose mutual interest in physical activity, ecology, conservation and the great outdoors evolved into an ever-widening circle of friends who call themselves the Weakenders. (TM)

## Acknowledgements:

Our sincere appreciation for the cooperation and assistance given by the Departments of Transportation and Natural Resources and the Office of Tourism of the State of Minnesota. Also the Division of Tourism and the Department of Natural Resources Bureau of Parks and Recreation of the State of Wisconsin.

We also acknowledge the cooperation and information provided by the many state, city and county parks and/or engineering departments whose assistance was invaluable in assembling many of the trail descriptions contained in this book.

### *In Celebration of Cycling*

*To wheel quietly up and down hill and across the valley, miles away from so-called civilization, and yet knowing that with a good bicycle miles mean but little; to wheel along drinking in the perfumes of the morning with the song of the birds, and at even, thankful for the matchless glow in the west and the music of cow-bells; to wheel silently at sunset into some peaceful village where your guidebook bids you expect a welcome — all this is worth celebrating.*

*Philip C. Hubert, Jr.*
*Scribners Magazine, 1895*

# Introduction:

Whether you are now a bicyclist, or about to become one, this book is for you. If you value friendships, good exercise, the outdoors or just economic transportation, you will find this guide a reliable reference to enhance your enjoyment.

Minnesota is the leader in the development of paved bicycle trails with over 600 miles now available to you. Wisconsin is not far behind.

The Minnesota and Wisconsin DNRs and Bureaus of Parks & Recreation have worked with interested communities and groups to convert railroad right-of-ways to bike trails, offering great biking that offers a quiet biking experience through scenic areas on level to minor grade rail beds.

Whatever your age or biking skill, whether you want to bike a short distance or several hours, this book is your guide to leisurely biking on safe trails, away from motorized traffic.

The trail maps, trail length and access information in this book tell you where to go, what to expect and how to get there.

# Contents

## GENERAL INFORMATION

The map below shows the location of the Minnesota and Wisconsin trails described within this book. See the following pages to view each quadrant of the state in more detail.

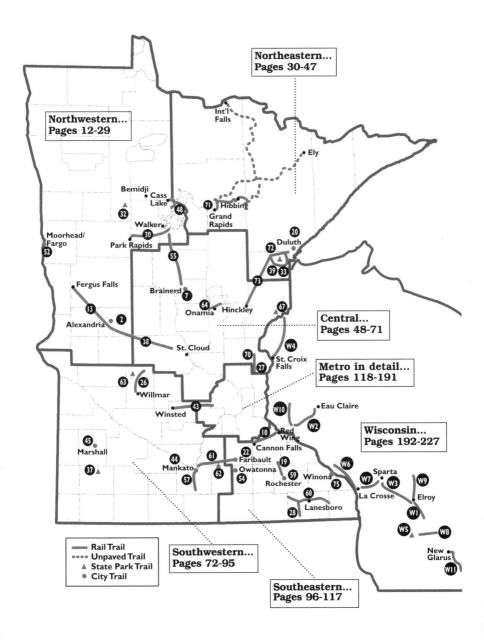

Northeastern...
Pages 30-47

Northwestern...
Pages 12-29

Int'l Falls

Ely

Bemidji
Cass Lake
32
Walker
30
Moorhead/Fargo
52
Park Rapids
55

71 Hibbing
Grand Rapids

48

20
72 Duluth

39 33
73

Fergus Falls
13
Alexandria
2

Brainerd
7
64 Hinckley
Onamia

67

Central...
Pages 48-71

38
St. Cloud

70
27
St. Croix Falls

W4

Metro in detail...
Pages 118-191

63 26
Willmar

Winsted

43

W10
Eau Claire

W2

Wisconsin...
Pages 192-227

45
Marshall

37

44
Mankato
57

61
62
54

10 Red Wing
22 Cannon Falls
Faribault
19
Owatonna
59 Winona
Rochester
75

W6
Sparta
W7 W3 W9
La Crosse Elroy
W1

60
28 Lanesboro

W5 W8

Rail Trail
Unpaved Trail
State Park Trail
City Trail

Southwestern...
Pages 72-95

New Glarus
W11

Southeastern...
Pages 96-117

11

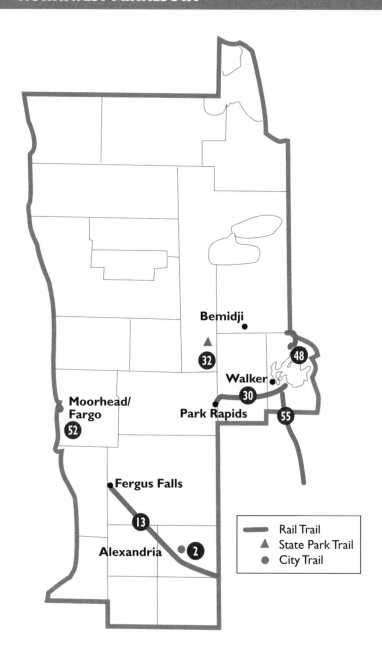

Bemidji

32

Walker

48

Moorhead/
Fargo

30

52

Park Rapids

55

Fergus Falls

13

Alexandria

2

| | Rail Trail |
| --- | --- |
| ▲ | State Park Trail |
| ● | City Trail |

# Northwest Minnesota

## Trail

**\* Numbers refer to large map on page 11 and opposite page**

**WHERE:** City of Alexandria
**LENGTH:** Several miles
**SURFACE:** Crushed rock through Polk County
**TRAIL USE:**

Alexandria has several miles of well marked roadside trails, specifically along county roads 22, 23 and 82. The city is also spanned east to west by the Central Lakes Rail-Trail (page 16) which will eventually run from Lake Wobegon Trail (page 52) in Sauk Centre all the way to Fergus Falls. Presently, the Central Lakes Trail is suitable for only snowmobiles or mountain bikes, but paving is planned.

### FOR MORE INFORMATION:

Alexandria Lakes Area Chamber of
  Commerce
206 Broadway
Alexandria, MN 56308
1-800-235-9441
E-Mail: alexrecr@rea-alp.com

Alexandria Lakes Community
  Recreation
P.O. Box 801
Alexandria, MN 56308
320-762-2868

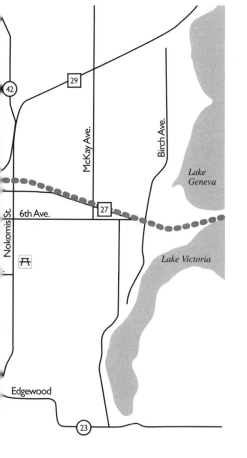

| | |
|---|---|
| Ⓟ | Parking |
| 🚻 | Restrooms |
| 🎋 | Picnic Area |
| ⛺ | Camping |
| ▬▬ | Paved Bike Trail |
| ●●● | Unpaved Trail |
| - - | On-road Trail |
| ◆ | Distance Marker |

**WHERE:** Osakis to Fergus Falls
**LENGTH:** 69 miles (when completed)
**SURFACE:** Crushed rock
**TRAIL USE:**

**Trailhead East:** Osakis at intersection of Hwy 27 and rail corridor adjacent to the Osakis Chamber of Commerce where there is parking.

**Mid Access:** Small towns along the route accessible from I-94 include Nelson, Garfield, Brandon, Evansville, Ashby and Dalton. The trail will traverse the entire city of Alexandria, east to west.

**Trailhead West:** Fergus Falls going north on I-94 exit 61 which is County Road 82. Proceed north to DeLagoon Park where there are facilities, parking and overnight camping

Mn DOT currently owns this right-of-way. The counties of Douglas, Grant and Otter Tail will construct and administer their sections just as is being done by Stearns County for the Lake Wobegon Trail to which this will eventually connect.

The surface is presently gravel suitable only for mountain bikes. Paving and parking, etc. will follow if projected maintenance costs do not prohibit it because of the reinstatement of studded snowmobiles.

This will rank very high on the list of most scenic rail-trails when completed. The rail bed winds its way along or near many lakes, streams and wooded areas.

### *FOR MORE INFORMATION:*

Central Lakes Trail Office
320-763-6001

Osakis Chamber of Commerce
P.O. Box 327
Osakis, MN 56360
320-859-3777

Fergus Falls Area Chamber of
  Commerce
202 S. Court St.
Fergus Falls, MN 56537
218-736-6951

Alexandria Lakes Area Chamber
  of Commerce
206 Broadway
Alexandria, MN 56308
800-235-9441

## Hand and arm signal methods

Left turn: left hand and arm extended horizontally

Right turn: hand and arm extended upward or extend right hand and arm horizontally to right side of bicycle

Stop or decrease speed: left hand and arm extended downward

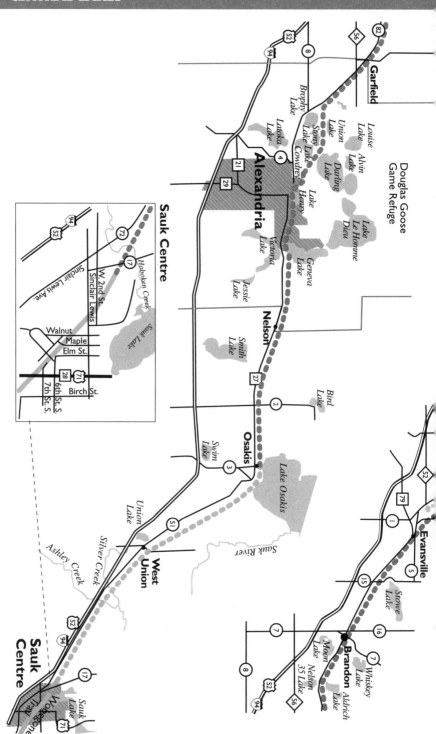

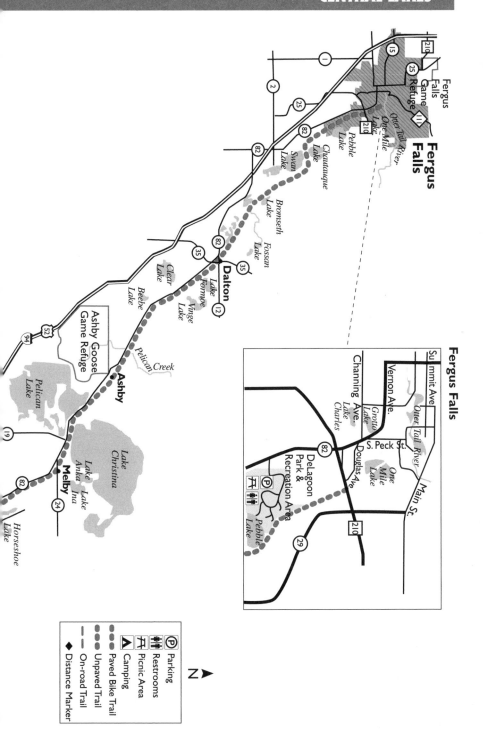

Fergus Falls

Fergus Falls Game Refuge

Otter Tail River

One-Mile Lake
Pebble Lake
Chautauque Lake
Swan Lake
Bromseth Lake
Fossan Lake
Clear Lake
Beebe Lake
Lake Fenroe
Vinge Lake
Dalton
Ashby Goose Game Refuge
Pelican Creek
Ashby
Pelican Lake
Lake Christina
Lake Anka
Lake Ina
Melby
Horseshoe Lake

**Fergus Falls**

Summit Ave.
Channing Ave.
Vernon Ave.
Otter Tail River
Main St.
Lake Charles
Grotto Lake
S. Peck St.
Delagoon Park & Recreation Area
Douglas Ave.
One Mile Lake
Pebble Lake

N ▶

**P** Parking
Restrooms
Picnic Area
Camping
Paved Bike Trail
Unpaved Trail
On-road Trail
◆ Distance Marker

**WHERE:** Park Rapids to Walker
**LENGTH:** 28 miles
**SURFACE:** Blacktop
**TRAIL USE:**

**Trailhead West:** The trail begins at Heartland Park in Park Rapids. Going east on Highway 34 through Park Rapids, you turn north on Central Avenue. There is a sign on Central Avenue indicating the Heartland Trail. You turn left (west) on North Street which leads right into the park. There is a large paved parking lot here, with excellent facilities. Overnight parking is permitted.

**Mid Access:** Dorset, Nevis and Akeley, just off Highway 34.

**Trailhead East:** In Walker, where Highway 371 intersects with County Road 12. The access is one-half mile west on County Road 12. The parking lot, with restrooms, is set back from the street.

If you enjoy the north woods, glacial lakes and flowing streams, you will like the Heartland Trail. The Trailhead West is located just 21 miles from one of the major attractions in northern Minnesota, Itasca State Park and the origin of the mighty Mississippi River.

Originally paved in 1975, this was the first blacktopped trail in Minnesota, perhaps in the country. The Heartland is a popular trail for snowmobilers in winter. The surfaced bike portions are part of many miles of trail for winter recreation which are not suitable for biking unless your are a real mountain bike enthusiast. These trails do, however, offer an opportunity to get off your bicycle and take a quiet walk in the woods.

The 28 miles of paved bike trail is an easy half-day ride through the Chippewa State Forest and also lends itself to a two-way, one day ride. Our group prefers to ride to Walker one day and back to Park Rapids the next. This is partly because of the driving distance from home, but also because of the interesting towns, scenery and the area in general. For overnight trips, reservations are highly recommended if you want a motel room during the tourist season.

If you plan to ride two days, we recommend starting at Heartland Park in Park Rapids where you may leave your car overnight. Heading east out of Park Rapids you will soon find yourself in deep woods with only an occasional farm field or residence in sight. About 10½ miles brings you into Nevis where you can have lunch.

Another 5½ miles puts you in Akeley, where you will want to ride one block off the trail and have your picture taken while sitting on the hand of a huge Paul Bunyan statue at the municipal park on Main Street. On the north side of the trail at Akeley, there is a picnic shelter, tables and restrooms. A well with hand pump will give you good water.

From Akeley to Walker is probably the most scenic section. You leave the proximity of Highway 34 (and an occasional residence) and ride by numerous lakes. The east end of the trail ends rather abruptly and it is necessary to ride the last one-quarter mile into Walker on city streets.

In Walker, we found excellent accommodations at reasonable rates and a family restaurant just a short distance from the marina on beautiful Leech Lake.

The entire trail from Park Rapids to Walker was resurfaced in 1997. Future plans include extending the trail from Walker to Cass Lake. The Paul Bunyan Trail, which now runs from Brainerd to Hackensack, will eventually intersect with the Heartland on its way to Bemidji.

Itasca State Park is just 21 miles north of Park Rapids. There are 17 miles of bike paths in the park (see page 24). Closer to Walker, the scenic and unfortunately named Leech Lake is located in Minnesota's beautiful Chippewa National Forest.

### FOR MORE INFORMATION:

Trail Office
P.O. Box 112
Nevis, MN 56467
218-652-4054

Leech Lake Area Chamber of
Commerce
P.O. Box 1089
Walker, MN 56484
218-547-1313
800-833-1118

Park Rapids Chamber of Commerce
Highway 71 South
P.O. Box 249
Park Rapids, MN 56470
800-247-0054

Bemidji Area Trails & Waterways
6603 Birchmont Beach Rd. N.
Bemidji, MN 56601
218-755-2265

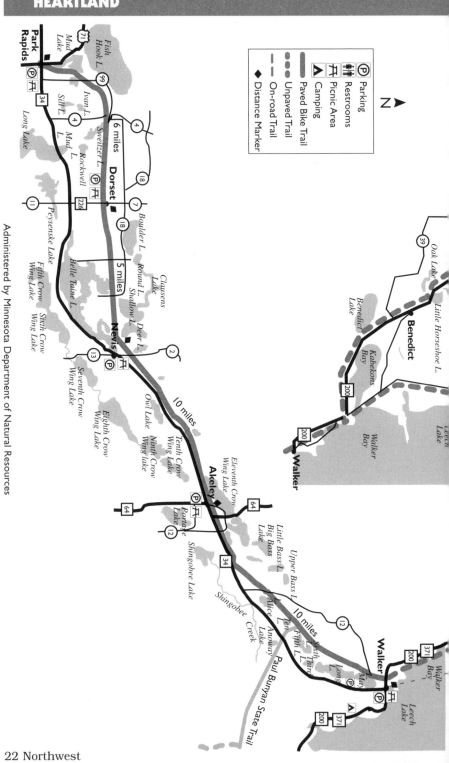

Administered by Minnesota Department of Natural Resources

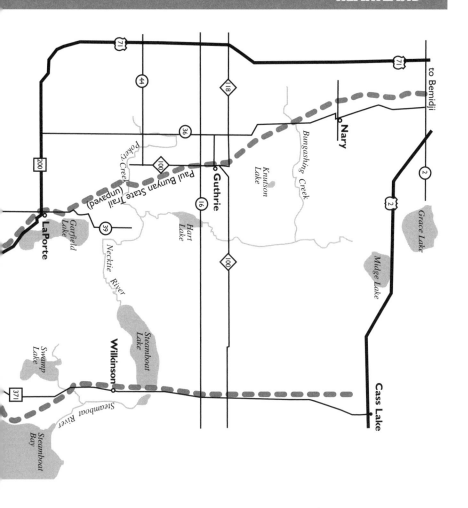

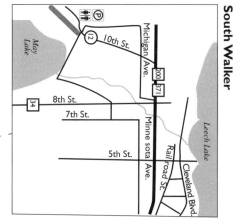

**South Walker**

**WHERE:** 21 miles north of Park Rapids on Highway 71
**LENGTH:** 17 miles, 6.5 miles off-road
**SURFACE:** Paved
**TRAIL USE:** 🚴 🚶 🛼 ✈ 🚣 🐎

Here is a chance to combine a really scenic bike ride with a visit to one of the more famous state parks in the nation. Not only is the scenery impressive, but the park offers a wide variety of other attractions. In 1991 this park celebrated its 100th birthday.

The off-road path is only 6.5 miles, with an additional 10.5 miles designated on low traffic roads. This permits a complete circle ride around Lake Itasca. Bike rentals are available in the park. The Trailhead South starts at the information center on the east entrance road, and the Trailhead North starts in the parking lot for the interpretive center at the headwaters of the Mississippi River near the north entrance road.

The location lends itself well to a companion trip with the Heartland Trail (see page 20). Biking enthusiasts may want to consider staying in Park Rapids or riding to Park Rapids. It is only 20 miles via U.S. Highway 71 from the south edge of the park. The highway has paved shoulders specifically marked for biking or hiking and it would be an interesting ride.

The virgin pines, lakes and other attractions of the park make this trail a real gem for outdoor enthusiasts and nature lovers. Be sure of your reservations, including campgrounds, during the summer season.

---

### *FOR MORE INFORMATION:*

Itasca State Park
HCO 5, Box 4
Lake Itasca, MN 56460
218-266-3654

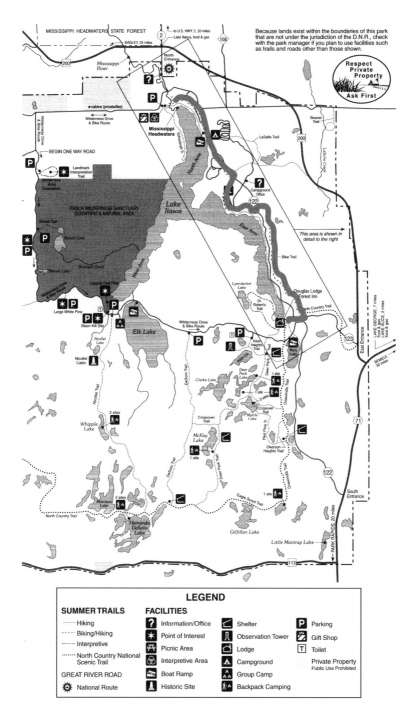

Because lands exist within the boundaries of this park that are not under the jurisdiction of the D.N.R., check with the park manager if you plan to use facilities such as trails and roads other than those shown.

Respect Private Property
Ask First

This area is shown in detail to the right

## LEGEND

### SUMMER TRAILS
- Hiking
- Biking/Hiking
- Interpretive
- North Country National Scenic Trail

GREAT RIVER ROAD
- National Route

### FACILITIES
- Information/Office
- Point of Interest
- Picnic Area
- Interpretive Area
- Boat Ramp
- Historic Site

- Shelter
- Observation Tower
- Lodge
- Campground
- Group Camp
- Backpack Camping

- Parking
- Gift Shop
- Toilet
- Private Property
  Public Use Prohibited

**WHERE:** Chippewa National Forest–Cass Lake
**LENGTH:** Approximately 3 miles (18 miles when complete)
**SURFACE:** Asphalt 8' wide, 10' wide through the campground
**TRAIL USE:** 🚲 🚶 🏊 🎿

**Trailhead North:** From the North, the Wanaki Campground and Knutsen Dam at north end of the Norway Beach recreation area on Cass Lake (open seasonally).

**Trailhead South:** The trail presently dead ends just over one-half mile south of Highway 2 on east side of Pike Bay. No parking at this point.

This is a new trail built and administered by the U.S. Forest Service. Although presently short, we include it here because of its future potential and its eventual connection with the city of Cass Lake and the Heartland Trail into Walker. Mi-ge-zi is Anishinabe for "Bald Eagle."

Although not constructed on a rail bed, this trail is flat and scenic, overlooking and/or adjacent to the shore of Cass Lake at frequent intervals. The trail passes through dense woods and large pines. This is especially true around the east side, and will also hold true of the south shore of Pike Bay when that section is completed.

The Chippewa National Forest also has many miles of paved road shoulders marked as bike routes, if you wish to extend your ride.

### FOR MORE INFORMATION:

Chippewa National Forest
Ranger Work Station
Route 3, Box 219
Cass Lake, MN 56633
218-335-8618

Chippewa National Forest
Ranger Station
HCR 73, Box 15
Walker, MN 56484
218-547-1044

Cass Lake Area Civic and
Commerce Association
PO Box 548
Cass Lake, MN 56633
218-335-6723 (season only)

Bemidji Area Chamber of Commerce
300 Bemidji Ave.
Bemidji, MN 56619
218-751-3541
800-458-2223

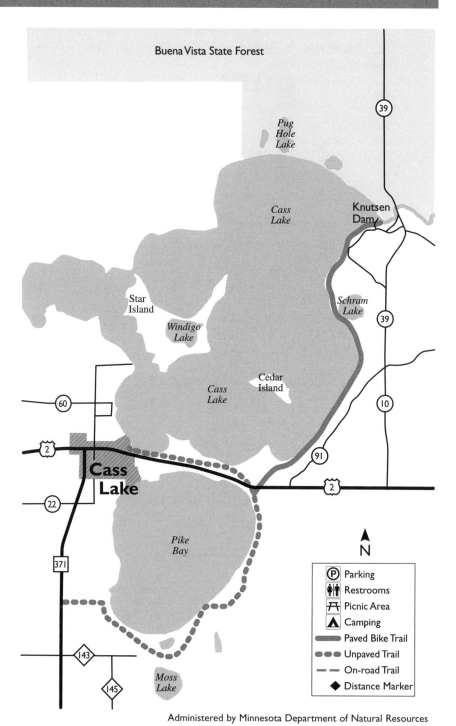

Buena Vista State Forest

Pug Hole Lake

Cass Lake

Knutsen Dam

Star Island

Windigo Lake

Schram Lake

Cedar Island

Cass Lake

Cass Lake

Pike Bay

Moss Lake

N

| | |
|---|---|
| Ⓟ | Parking |
| 🚹🚺 | Restrooms |
| ⛱ | Picnic Area |
| ⛺ | Camping |
| ▬ | Paved Bike Trail |
| ●●● | Unpaved Trail |
| – – | On-road Trail |
| ◆ | Distance Marker |

Administered by Minnesota Department of Natural Resources

**WHERE:** Cities of Moorhead and Fargo
**LENGTH:** Moorhead-12.5 miles, Fargo-25 miles
**SURFACE:** Paved
**TRAIL USE:** 🚴 🚶 🎿 ⛷️

Both Moorhead and Fargo have quite extensive dedicated bicycle and recreational trails along with on-street trails. Both cities take advantage of the scenery and green space provided by the Red River of the North which divides the two cities. Dedicated trails also continue east from Moorhead into Dilworth along Highway 10.

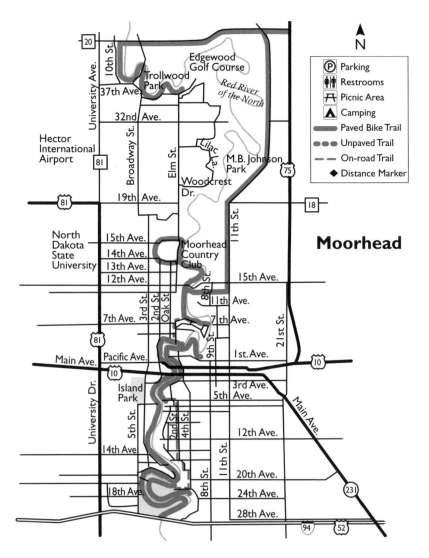

# Fargo

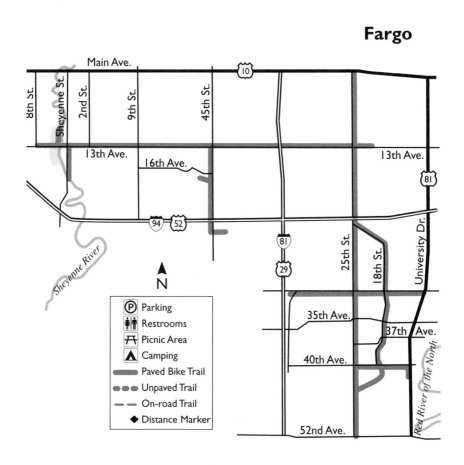

**Legend:**
- Ⓟ Parking
- 🚻 Restrooms
- ⛏ Picnic Area
- ⛺ Camping
- Paved Bike Trail
- ●●● Unpaved Trail
- — — On-road Trail
- ◆ Distance Marker

---

### FOR MORE INFORMATION:

Fargo/Moorhead
Chamber of Commerce
P.O. Box 2443
Fargo, ND 58108
701-237-5678

Moorhead Parks Department
324-24th St. S.
Moorhead, MN 56560
218-299-5340

Fargo Parks Department
P.O. Box 1796
Fargo, ND 58107
701-241-1350

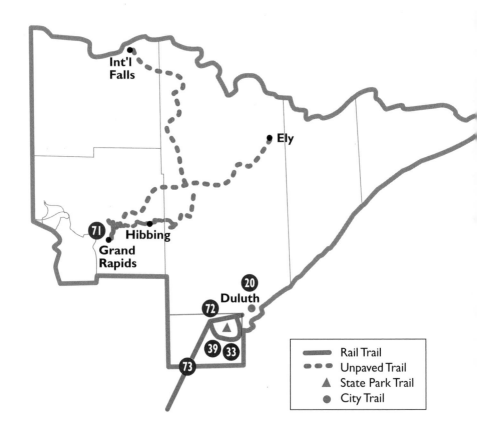

Int'l
Falls

Ely

Hibbing

71

Grand
Rapids

20

Duluth

72

39 33

73

| | Rail Trail |
| --- | --- |
| | Unpaved Trail |
| ▲ | State Park Trail |
| ● | City Trail |

# Northeast Minnesota

## Trail

\* **Numbers refer to large map on page 11 and opposite page**

**WHERE:** City of Duluth
**LENGTH:** Trails range from 1.5 miles-23 miles
**SURFACE:** Varies between trails
**TRAIL USE:** 🚲 🚶 🛼

**Access:** Canal Park and off several city streets (see maps).

There are several bike routes in the Duluth-Superior area in addition to the Willard Munger Trail which you can follow some 65 miles to Hinckley (see page 46) and the Alex Laveau Memorial Trail (see page 36) which travels to Wrenshall. Lakewalk (see below) is a very popular path located next to Lake Superior and the busy Canal Park area. A section of this 3-mile trail has a boardwalk for pedestrians and an asphalt trail for bikers and skaters. Western Waterfront Trail (next page) is unpaved and about 5 miles long with the portion designated for bicycling shown on the map. Trails and paths you may want to consider that we haven't mapped include Central Entrance Bicycle Path (near Central High School, about 1.5 miles long), Bong Bridge Path (about 2.5 miles long, crossing the St. Louis Bay next to the Bridge's eastbound lane), and the Osaugie Trail (multi-purpose trail next to State Highway 53 in Superior). You can also bike along some 21 miles of the North Shore Drive by following the designated bike route signs. In addition, numerous scenic parks in town have hiking and cross-country ski trails, and nearby Jay Cooke State Park (see page 34) also has beautiful trails.

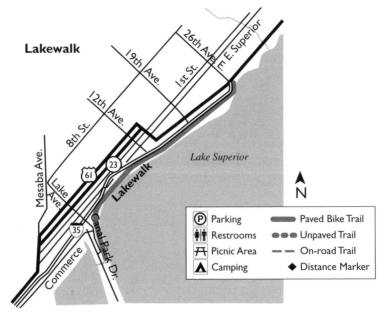

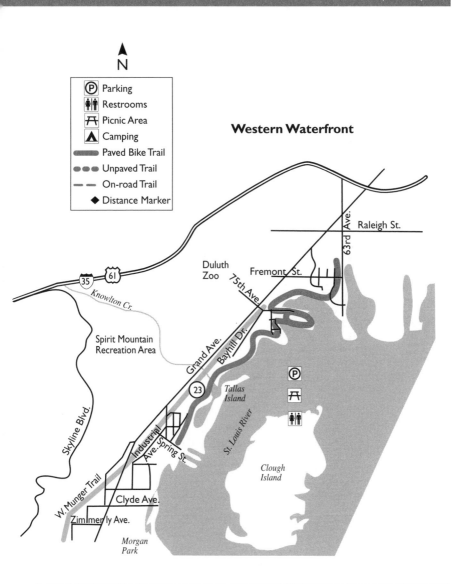

**Western Waterfront**

Parking
Restrooms
Picnic Area
Camping
Paved Bike Trail
Unpaved Trail
On-road Trail
Distance Marker

N

Raleigh St.
63rd Ave.
Duluth Zoo
Fremont St.
75th Ave.
Knowlton Cr.
Spirit Mountain Recreation Area
Grand Ave.
Bayhill Dr.
Tallas Island
St. Louis River
Clough Island
Skyline Blvd.
Industrial Ave.
Spring St.
W. Munger Trail
Clyde Ave.
Zimmerly Ave.
Morgan Park

## FOR MORE INFORMATION:

Duluth CVB
Endion Station
100 Lake Place Drive
Duluth, MN 55802
218-722-4011
1-800-438-5884
www.visitduluth.com

Parks and Recreation
330 City Hall
Duluth, MN 55802
218-723-3612

**WHERE:** Carlton
**LENGTH:** 3 miles
**SURFACE:** Paved roadside only within park
**TRAIL USE:** 🚴 🚶 📷 🏊 ⛷

**Access:** Park entrance is off Hiway 210, 3 miles east of Carlton.

Although there are very few separate bicycle trails within the park, it is an excellent base for a bicycle outing. It is surrounded on all four sides by state rail-trails and/or improved roadside lanes. The Munger from Carlton to Duluth traverses the north side, and the Alex Laveau skirts the west, south and east sides.

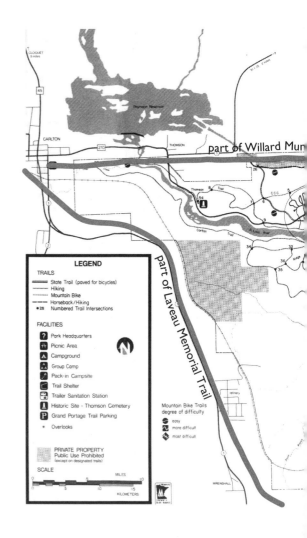

**FOR MORE INFORMATION:**

Jay Cooke State Park
500 E. Highway 210
Carlton, MN 55718
218-384-4610

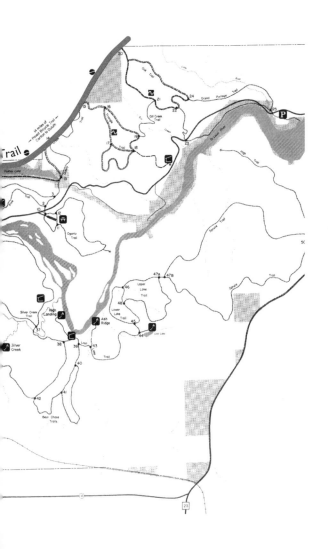

**WHERE:** Carlton to Duluth
**LENGTH:** 6 miles to Highway 23, 12 miles from Highway 23 into S. Duluth
**SURFACE:** Paved 10' wide on rail bed to Highway 23, paved road shoulder from Highway 23 into Duluth.
**TRAIL USE:**

**Trailhead West:** Carlton, 1 block south of Carlton Depot and the Munger Trail.

**Mid Access:** Wrenshall, off County Road 1.

**Trailhead North:** South Duluth. Via paved street shoulders, the Laveau presently joins the Munger at the bridge over Commonwealth Avenue (also Highway 23), but they will eventually intersect at Beaudry Street.

Utilizing the Munger State Trail, this new addition provides an excellent circle route for a total ride of just over 35 miles. This trail will give you a different view of Jay Cooke State Park and the St. Louis River Estuary in South Duluth.

This trail is somewhat unique in that the Carlton to Highway 23 segment is owned by the DNR, and the construction from the Highway 23 trail into Duluth is the combined effort of the MN DOT, Carlton, St. Louis counties and the City of Duluth.

The DNR portion follows an old rail bed from Carlton through Wrenshall and on to Highway 23. From that point, the DOT portion is a wide paved shoulder following Highway 23 into South Duluth.

The trail name honors the memory of a former County Commissioner and dairy farmer who was a strong advocate of the idea of reusing abandoned railways as public trails.

### FOR MORE INFORMATION:

DNR Trail Office
Route 2, 701 S. Kenwood
Moose Lake, MM
218-485-5410

Duluth Area Visitors Bureau
800-4-DULUTH

Duluth Area Chamber of Commerce
118 E. Superior St.
Duluth, MN 55802
218-722-5501

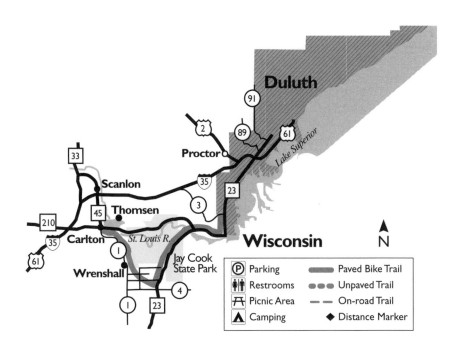

Administered by Minnesota Department of Natural Resources

---

## Bike Shorts

If you are not fully familiar with the area or trail you plan to ride, a good map or bicycle guide book can be very important. Not all trails and routes are well marked.

**Mesabi Trail** (see map page 44)
>**WHERE:** Grand Rapids to Ely
>**LENGTH:** 132 miles when completed
>**SURFACE:** bituminous, 10-14 feet wide
>**TRAIL USE:**

**Itasca Bicycle Trail** (see map page 40)
>**WHERE:** Grand Rapids to Gunn Park
>**LENGTH:** 6 miles
>**SURFACE:** Paved
>**TRAIL USE:**

**Arrowhead Trail** (no detailed map included)
>**WHERE:** Tower to International Falls
>**LENGTH:** 128 miles
>**SURFACE:** unimproved
>**TRAIL USE:**

**Taconite Trail** (see map page 40)
>**WHERE:** Grand Rapids to Ely
>**LENGTH:** 165 miles
>**SURFACE:** 5 miles paved
>**TRAIL USE:**

While the Taconite and Itasca Trails are coordinated and administered by the DNR, the Mesabi Trails is coordinated and administered by the St. Louis and Lake Counties Regional Railroad Authority, implementing plans some of which go as far back as the 1970s. They have undertaken an ambitious project to connect the population centers of this sparsely settled region and the combined efforts of city, county, state and private industry is gradually getting it done. Approximately 40% will be on rail bed.

Three of the trails (Mesabi, Itasca and Taconite) begin as one trail at the fairgrounds in Grand Rapids and continue for 3½ miles north to the Prairie River Dam. At that point, the Itasca Trail goes another 2 miles west to Gunn Park (open seasonally). The Taconite and Mesabi trails take two different routes to the east to Tower, where the Arrowhead goes north to International Falls. The Mesabi and Taconite proceed to Ely.

The Taconite and Arrowhead Trails are winter snowmobile trails with many parts unusable in summer. The Itasca Trail is paved for all of its 6 miles and the Mesabi Trail to date has paved and completed segments totaling approximately 55 miles.

International Falls

**Arrowhead Trail**

Ely

Tower

**Taconite Trail**

**Mesabi Trail**

**Itasca Trail**

Hibbing

Grand Rapids

Duluth

## FOR MORE INFORMATION:

DNR
1201 East Highway 2
Grand Rapids, MN 55744
218-327-4408

Mesabi
St. Louis and Lake Counties Regional
 Railroad Authority
US Bank Place Suite 6B
230 First Street South
Virginia, MN 55792
218-749-0697

DNR
Box 388
406 Main St.
Tower, MN 55790
218-753-6257

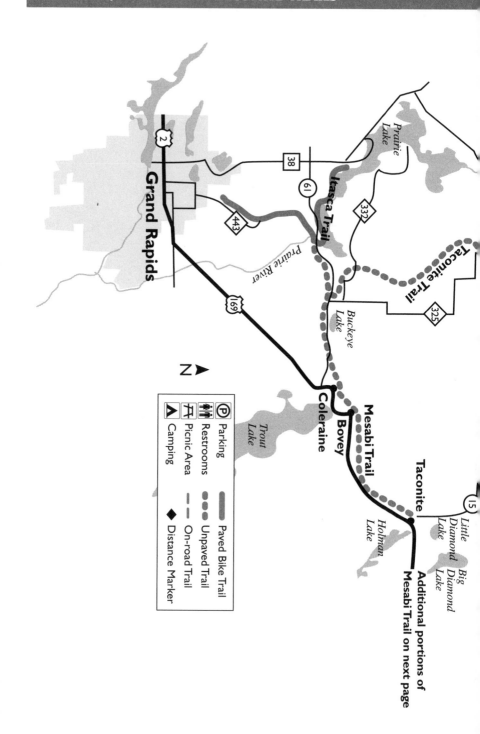

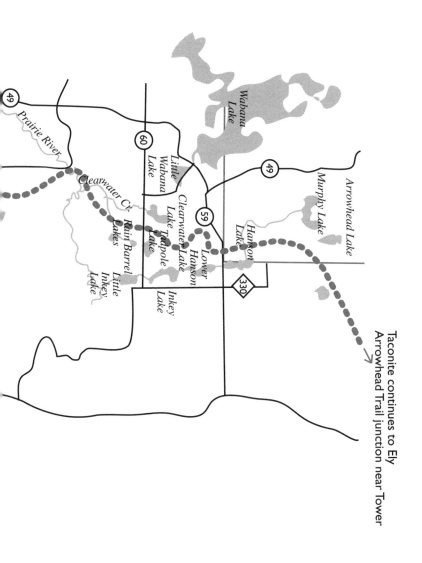

Wabana Lake

Little Wabana Lake

Clearwater Cr.

Clearwater Lake

Prairie River

Rain Barrel Lakes

Little Inkey Lake

Tadpole Lake

Inkey Lake

Lower Hanson Lake

Hanson Lake

Murphy Lake

Arrowhead Lake

Taconite continues to Ely
Arrowhead Trail junction near Tower

### The Mesabi Trail

This will be a 132-mile, multi-use recreational trail linking over 22 communities across the Iron Range area. Utilizing abandoned railways, logging and mine haul roads and existing bike trails, the trail will provide safe and healthy recreational opportunities.

The trail alignment will emphasize the historic, scenic, environmental and educational aspects of the region while providing alternate transportation possibilities for local communities. Along the trail will be learning centers where users can stop to learn about the forest, area geology and the region's fascinating history. The trail will be routed past established tourist attractions, where feasible.

The Mesabi Trail is destined to become a star quality attraction to the tourism industry and give an economic boost to the entire region. The estimated cost to complete this entire system is $10 million. Completion of the 132-mile length will be determined by funding availability.

The Mesabi Trail is a brand new trail and therefore the access points and descriptions that follow are tentative, pending further trail development. By the time of this printing, the following sections of the Mesabi will be paved and will allow biking and hiking. Please consult the Regional Railroad Authority at the address/phone number below for current trail status.

### Grand Rapids to Taconite Segment

**WHERE:** Grand Rapids to Taconite
**LENGTH:** 13 miles

**Trailhead West:** Grand Rapids Fairgrounds. From combined Hwys. 169 and 2, turn north onto 3rd Ave. NE to Itasca County Fairgrounds. Trail access at north side of fairgrounds.

**Mid Access:** Coleraine. From Hwy. 169, exit onto Curley Ave., trail access at intersection with Curley Ave. and Cole St. Bovey. From Hwy. 169 exit onto 2nd St (west) go one block to 1st. Ave., trail on left.

**Trailhead East:** Taconite. From Hwy. 169, exit onto Cty. 15 into town. Turn left on Haines Ave. to Community Center. Trail access at the Community Center.

## Nashwauk to Kinney Segment

**WHERE:** Nashwauk to Kinney
**LENGTH:** 28 miles

**Trailhead West:** Nashwauk. From Hwy.169 exit on Cty. 65. Continue north 7 blocks to the city park where you will find the trail access.

**Mid Access:** Keewatin. From Hwy. 169 exit Cty. 82 (7th St.). Continue north about .3 of a mile. Trail access at corner of 3rd Ave. and 7th St. Hibbing. From Hwy. 169 take Howard St. exit, and follow to 3rd Ave. E (Greyhound Blvd.). Turn right and continue 1 mile, trail on right. Chisholm. Exit Hwy. 169 onto 4th Ave. SE (downtown exit). Trail access on right about 150 feet from Highway.

**Trailhead East:** Kinney. From Hwy. 169 exit onto Hwy. 25 North. Continue .75 mile, with the trail access on left.

## Mt. Iron to Gilbert

**WHERE:** Mt. Iron to Gilbert
**LENGTH:** 11 miles

**Trailhead West:** Mt. Iron. From Hwy. 169 exit at Cty. 102 toward downtown. Trail access about .1 of a mile on right.

**Mid Access:** Virginia. From Hwy. 53 exit onto 9th St. North, travel 1.5 miles to 3rd St., and turn left. Trail access one block on left.

**Trailhead East:** Gilbert. From Hwy. 53, exit onto Hwy. 135 to Gilbert. Continue 3 miles to intersection of Hwy. 37 (Broadway), turn left. Trail access on right.

## Gilbert to Ely

Small sections are completed but most of this segment is still under construction.

---

### FOR MORE INFORMATION:

Mesabi
St. Louis and Lake Counties Regional Railroad Authority
US Bank Place Suite 6B
230 First Street South
Virginia, MN 55792
218-749-0697

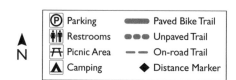

| | | | |
|---|---|---|---|
| ⓟ Parking | | ▬▬▬ | Paved Bike Trail |
| 🚻 Restrooms | | ●●● | Unpaved Trail |
| ⛩ Picnic Area | | – – – | On-road Trail |
| ⛺ Camping | | ◆ | Distance Marker |

N

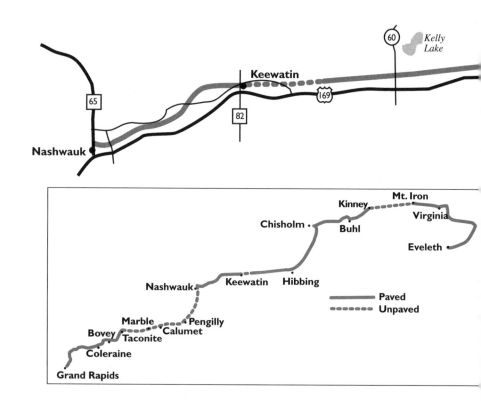

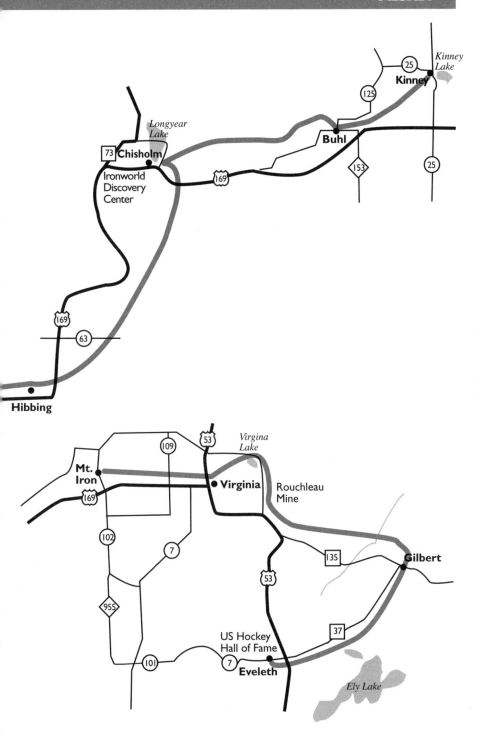

**WHERE:** Carlton to West Duluth
**LENGTH:** 14.5 miles
**SURFACE:** Paved
**TRAIL USE:** 🚴 🚶 📷 ➔

**Trailhead North:** Driving north on I-35, take Cody Street exit (251-A). Turn right on 63rd (south), you will intersect with Grand Avenue. The trail access is directly behind the Willard Motel at 75th Avenue and Grand Avenue. Also, at this location, you will see the Lake Superior Zoological Garden on the west side of Grand. Parking is available at the trail access. If driving south on I-35, take the Grand Avenue exit (S-23).

**Trailhead West:** Exit from I-35, on Highway 210, and drive east to Carlton. At the four-way stop, turn onto County Road 1, and proceed about one block south to the trail access depot and parking lot.

The Carlton to West Duluth segment is the very northern 14½ miles of what is eventually planned to be a single trail from St. Paul to Duluth (and perhaps beyond). Now completed and paved from Duluth to Hinckley, we have a super 68 mile distance ride.

The first time we selected this trail, we started at Duluth. While 14½ miles makes an easy two-way ride, the first 9 miles seem more of an uphill grade than the 3% slope. We recommend starting in Duluth so you can do that section while you are still fresh and because it permits you to start and end your ride in Duluth. While the ride up is a bit strenuous, the long coast back down makes up for it.

Along the way, there are some interesting cuts through solid rock, a great view of Lake Superior and Wisconsin, and other scenic vistas. The trail takes you through woods, alongside Jay Cooke State Park and over a high bridge overlooking a spectacular gorge where you may see park visitors swimming and fishing. We did not join them, but not much further west, we did cool off by wading into a cool, clear stream paralleling our path. One pleasant surprise en route was a mobile refreshment stand run by an enterprising individual complete with ice cream, pop, candy, food and picnic tables.

If you choose a one-way ride, there is ample parking one block from downtown Carlton. Because of the long down grade, you will find the Carlton to Duluth ride will take quite a bit less time so you may want to include a side trip into Jay Cooke State Park or ride the Laveau Memorial Bike Trail.

Also of interest along the way are the National Kayak School in Thomson, Whitewater rafting opportunities near Cloquet, and the Black Bear Casino, in Carlton. Finally, The Alex Laveau Memorial Bike trail access is just one block south of the Willard Munger depot trail access in Carlton. (See page 70).

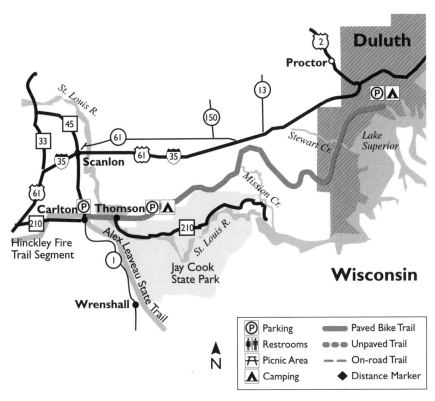

Administered by Minnesota Department of Natural Resources

### FOR MORE INFORMATION:

DNR Trail Office
Route 2, 701 S. Kenwood
Moose Lake, MN 55767
218-485-5410

Duluth Visitors Bureau
1-800-4-DULUTH

Duluth Area Chamber of Commerce
118 E. Superior St.
Duluth, MN 55802
218-722-5501

Western Waterfront Trail
Duluth Park and Recreation
218-723-3337

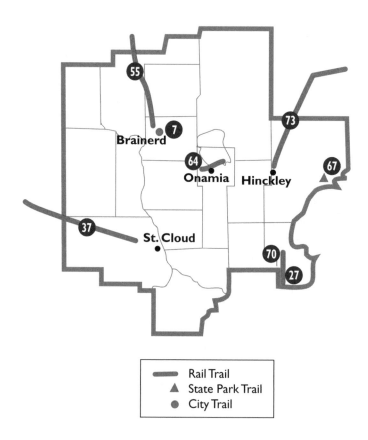

Rail Trail
State Park Trail
City Trail

# Central Minnesota

Trail

**\* Numbers refer to large map on page 11 and opposite page**

**WHERE:** City of Brainerd
**LENGTH:** Several miles
**SURFACE:** Paved
**TRAIL USE:**

The City of Brainerd has some excellent off-road and roadside trails. Its proximity to the south trailhead of the northbound Paul Bunyan DNR trail (see page 56) make this an excellent location for a bicycle outing.

There are many attractions and historic sites in the Brainerd Lakes Area including the Brainerd International Raceway, the Paul Bunyan Amusement Center, miniature golf courses or some 450 holes of golf, including several championship courses.

Over 465 sand bottom lakes within a 30-mile radius of Brainerd are very popular for boating, canoeing and fishing in the summer, cross-country skiing, snowmobiling and ice fishing in the winter.

### FOR MORE INFORMATION:

Brainerd Lakes Area C/CVB
124 North 6th Street
Brainerd, MN 56401
218-829-2838 ext. 483
www.brainerd.com

Parks and Recreation
1619 N.E. Washington
Brainerd, MN 56401
218-828-2320

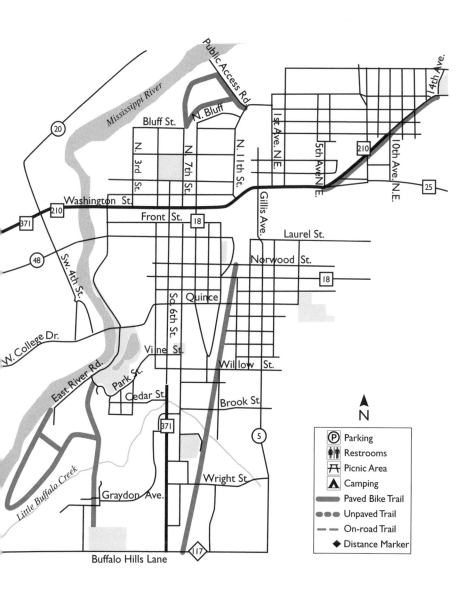

**WHERE:** Sauk Centre to Avon
**LENGTH:** 28 miles
**SURFACE:** Asphalt, 10' wide
**TRAIL USE:** 🚴 🚶 ♿ 🏊

**Trailhead East:** Avon, with a soon to be paved parking lot just across County Road 9 in downtown Avon. Facilities also planned. Exit I-94 at Highway 157 or 9.

**Mid Access:** Albany, with parking on Second Street. Melrose and Freeport exits from I-94.

**Trailhead West:** Sauk Centre. There is parking and access on city streets, but presently there is none at the actual pavement end on Highway 17 in west Sauk Centre. Funds have been secured for a connecting off-road spur from Highway 17 on the west to the city park at the south end of Sauk Lake. This will be the actual trailhead and provide parking, facilities and camping when completed.

The Lake Wobegon Trail was dedicated in September 1998. It was built and is managed by Stearns County Parks Department. It received its name by special permission from Garrison Keillor who located his fictional lake in this area. Financed with an ISTEA Grant, local donations and some DNR funds, this is an excellent addition to Minnesota's trail system.

It is by far the best marked trail we have ridden, with mile markers every one-half mile and warning signs in advance of every stop sign. It is also unique to us to find smooth asphalt paved bridges. Much of the local fund-raising as well as the impetus to build the trail was provided by the Albany Jaycees and each community enthusiastically supports it. This includes a neat rest stop with special tables beside the trail in Melrose provided by a local businessman.

---

### FOR MORE INFORMATION:

Lake Wobegon Regional Trail
Trail Office
Stearns County Parks
455-28th Ave. S.
Waite Park, MN 56387
320-255-6172

Sauk Centre Chamber of Commerce
1220 S. Main St.
P.O. Box 222
Sauk Centre, MN 56378
320-352-5201

Melrose Chamber of Commerce
407 E. Main
Melrose, MN 56352
320-245-7174

Albany Chamber of Commerce
P.O. Box 634
Albany, MN 56307
320-845-7777

A municipal building is under construction in Albany which will provide parking and facilities. The right-of-way has been secured for an eventual continuation all the way to Fergus Falls on the west with a rail bed connection into St. Cloud on the east also a possibility.

This is mostly an open rail-trail with very few country roads crossing it. However, the close proximity of I-94 along most of the route does little to promote serenity and this is mostly an open rail-trail. Consider wind direction when you plan your ride. We found the first 6 miles out of Avon to be the most sheltered and scenic, but don't miss the Sinclair Lewis Interpretive Center in Sauk Centre near the I-94 exit to Highway 71 and 28.

*New Trail headquarters and City Hall at Albany*

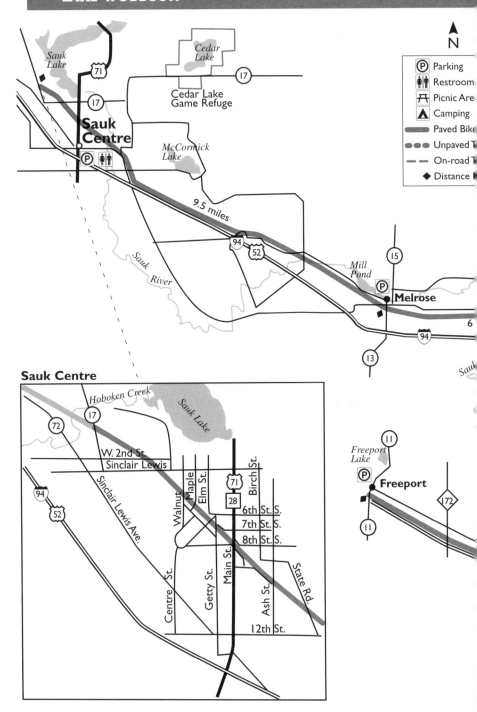

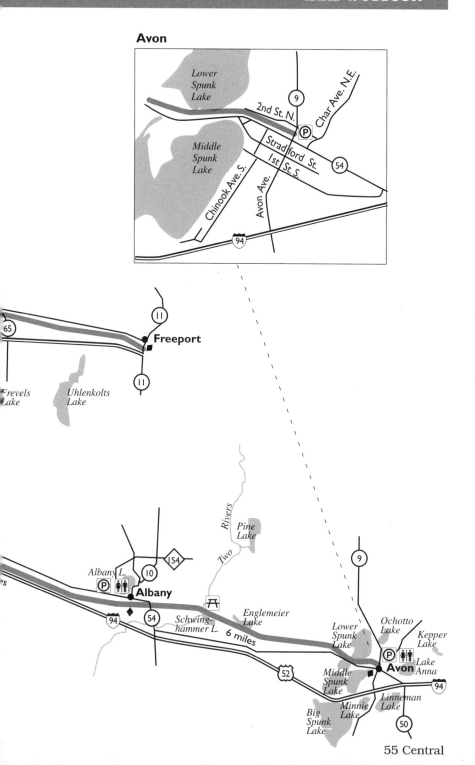

**Avon**

Lower Spunk Lake

Middle Spunk Lake

2nd St. N.

Char Ave. N.E.

Stradford St.

1st St. S.

Chinook Ave. S.

Avon Ave.

94

Freeport

65

Frevels Lake

Uhlenkolts Lake

Rivers

Pine Lake

Two

Albany L.

154

10

Albany

94

54

Schwing-hammer L.

6 miles

Englemeier Lake

Lower Spunk Lake

Ochotto Lake

Kepper Lake

52

Middle Spunk Lake

Minnie Lake

Linneman Lake

Lake Anna

Avon

94

Big Spunk Lake

50

**WHERE:** Baxter to Hackensack
**LENGTH:** 46.4 miles
**SURFACE:** Blacktop 10' wide
**TRAIL USE:** 🚲 🧍 🛼 ➡ 🏃

**Trailhead North:** Currently the paved trail terminates at Hackensack. The DNR has yet to complete the connection between Hackensack and the Heartland State Trail just southwest of Walker where the two trails will meet.

**Trailhead South:** Baxter. From Brainerd, go west on State Highway 210 about three-quarter miles. Turn north (right) on State Highway 371 to the first stoplight (Excelsior Rd). Turn east (right) and continue to the parking lot adjacent to the Paul Bunyan Arboretum.

**Mid Access:** At Merrifield, which is 9 miles north of Baxter. There is parking at the public access for North Long Lake, where you will find various resorts and businesses. Nisswa, Pequot Lakes, Jenkins, Pine River and Backus all offer parking, resorts, businesses and city parks. Presently, the trail terminates at Hackensack, paralleling Highway 371. Be sure to watch for signs. Parking and city facilities are available here.

Completed from Baxter/Brainerd to Hackensack in 1995, this DNR trail lies along an historic rail bed from the lumbering heydays of northern Minnesota. The trail generally parallels Highway 371 (particularly through the towns) but provides frequent views and accesses to lakes and wetlands for which Minnesota is famous.

The emphasis of this trail is on the pine forests, lakes and wetlands of North Central Minnesota, along with its wildlife, fishing and other recreational opportunities. It is a great addition to the upper Midwest rail-trail system.

In addition to numerous lakes and wetlands, the area traveled has tourist attractions such as well-known resorts (i.e. Grand View Lodge), Nisswa, the Hay Lake Mound District (a Native American burial ground near Jenkins), and the Paul Bunyan Arboretum, which is very near the trail's beginning in Baxter. There is a photo opportunity of Paul Bunyan's girlfriend at Hackensack and of course, Paul Bunyan and Babe, his Blue Ox, in Baxter. There are many fishing and swimming opportunities on this trail. Accommodations of all kinds abound in the resort area, with large and small resort communities located at reasonable intervals throughout.

Although there will be some interruptions, the rail bed from Hackensack to Bemidji is already secured assuring an eventual 100 mile trail which will showcase northern Minnesota attractions. Plans include connecting to the Heartland State Trail west of Walker (see page 20) as well as other points north from Walker and Bemidji. Someday Walker may be a central point for some very extensive bicycle trail riding.

## Bike Shorts

Yield the right-of-way to vehicles or pedestrians. Be prepared to do so even if you have the right-of-way. A bicycle is hardly the vehicle for practicing that a good offense is the best defense.

### FOR MORE INFORMATION:

DNR Trail Office
1601 Minnesota Drive
Brainerd, MN 56401
218-828-2693

Brainerd Chamber of Commerce
P.O. Box 356
Brainerd, MN 56401
218-829-2838
800-450-2838

Nisswa Chamber of Commerce
549 Main St.
P.O. Box 185
Nisswa, MN 56468
218-963-2620
800-950-9610

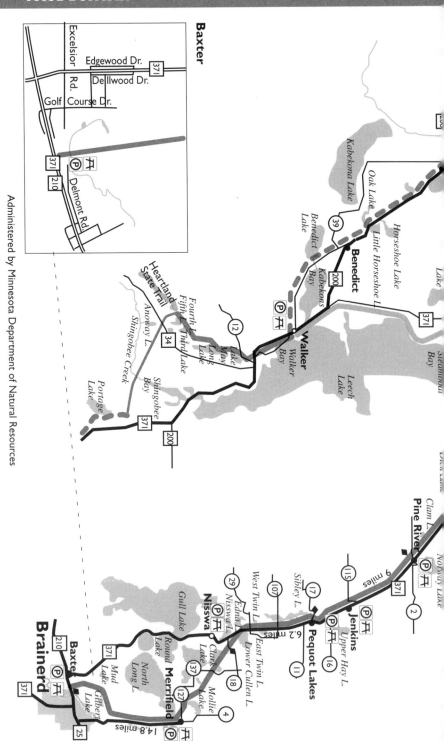

Baxter

Excelsior Rd.
Edgewood Dr.
Dellwood Dr.
Golf Course Dr.
37
210
Delmont Rd.

Administered by Minnesota Department of Natural Resources

Kabekona Lake
Oak Lake
Little Horseshoe Bay
Horseshoe Lake
Little Horseshoe L.
Benedict Lake
39
Benedict
200
Kabekona Bay
371

Heartland State Trail
Fourth L.
Fifth L. Third Lake
34
12
May Lake
Long Lake
Anoway L.
Shingobee Creek
Walker
Walker Bay
Leech Lake
Portage Lake
Shingobee Bay
37
200

Steamboat Bay
Lake

Clam L.
Pine River
Norway Lake
371
2

9 miles
115
Jenkins
16
Upper Hay L.
17
Sibley L.
Pequot Lakes
11
29
West Twin L.
107
East Twin L.
Lower Cullen L.
6.2 miles
Nisswa
Edna L.
Nisswa L.
Clark Lake
18
37
Mollie Lake
127
4
Merrifield
Gull Lake
Round Lake
North Long L.
Mud Lake
371
210
Baxter
Brainerd
Gilbert Lake
14.8 miles
25
371

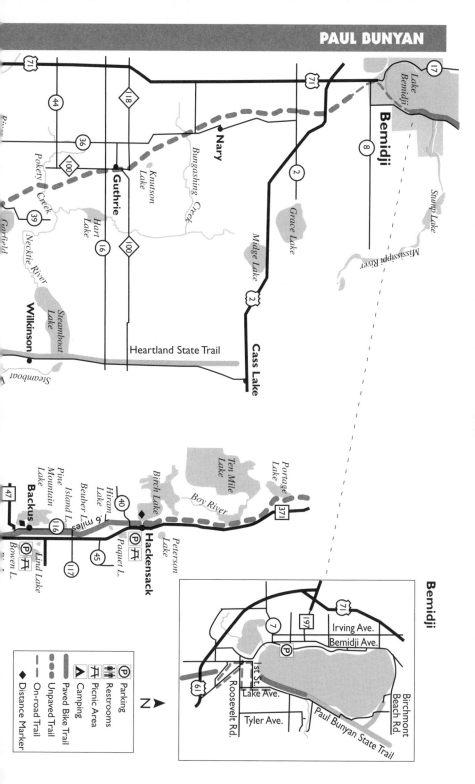

Legend:
- Ⓟ Parking
- ⛨ Restrooms
- ⛺ Camping
- ⛼ Picnic Area
- ▲ Camping
- Paved Bike Trail
- Unpaved Trail
- On-road Trail
- ◆ Distance Marker

N ➤

**WHERE:** Onamia to Isle
**LENGTH:** 11 miles
**SURFACE:** Paved, 8' wide
**TRAIL USE:**

**Trailhead West:** At Onamia, at the depot on Pike St. where there is parking available. The trail actually extends one-quarter mile west to 125th Avenue.

**Mid Access:** At Wahkon, County Road 17, south end of Main Street.

**Trailhead East:** At Isle, follow 17 one block south of business district to the ball park, where parking is available. You may choose to follow green bike route signs west of the ball park to Father Hennepin State Park.

Opened in the spring of 1995, this new trail is located just 90 miles north of the Twin Cities. It was developed by Mille Lacs County on the old Soo Line rail bed and is the first phase of a project that will eventually link Kathio State Park northwest of Onamia with Father Hennepin State Park east of Lake Mille Lacs. The goal is to provide a continuous bike, snowmobile and ATV path from one State Park to the other. Presently, one can connect to Kathio State Park from Onamia via County roads and to Father Hennepin State Park via 4 blocks of Isle city streets.

The trail follows a straight line between Onamia and Isle, and is very flat. Much of it is through open farmland so wind might be a factor. A note of caution: this trail is also open to ATV travel so watch for motorized traffic.

The Soo Line Trail is an 11-mile segment, part of the 100-mile Genola-Superior snowmobile trail. The beginning of the trail at Genola is located on Highway 25 by the lumber yard. It is narrow, single file and the surface suitable for mountain bikes. Genola is approximately 20 miles west of Onamia via the trail.

For more recreational activities, you might consider the two local state parks, Father Hennepin and Kathio, in addition to Lake Mille Lacs, with its many resorts.

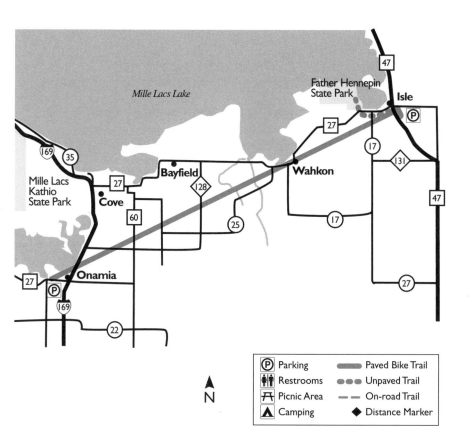

Mille Lacs Lake

Father Hennepin State Park

Isle

Bayfield

Wahkon

Mille Lacs Kathio State Park

Cove

Onamia

N

| | | | |
|---|---|---|---|
| (P) Parking | | Paved Bike Trail |
| Restrooms | | Unpaved Trail |
| Picnic Area | | On-road Trail |
| Camping | ◆ | Distance Marker |

**FOR MORE INFORMATION:**

Mille Lacs Bureau of Tourism
565 Eighth St. N.E.
Milaca, MN 56353
320-983-8201
800-350-2692

**WHERE:** Hinckley
**LENGTH:** 5.5 miles
**SURFACE:** Paved
**TRAIL USE:** 🚲 🥾 🏕 🎿 🐴

**Access:** 16 miles east of Hinckley on State Highway 48.

The largest state park in Minnesota also contains one of the longer paved trails. During the ride, you will see lots of woods and several streams. The park offers the most complete facilities of any Minnesota State Park. Also included within the park is a canoe rental concession which is extremely popular as is a river boat tour operation nearby. Fishing, swimming and camping all take advantage of the scenic St. Croix River.

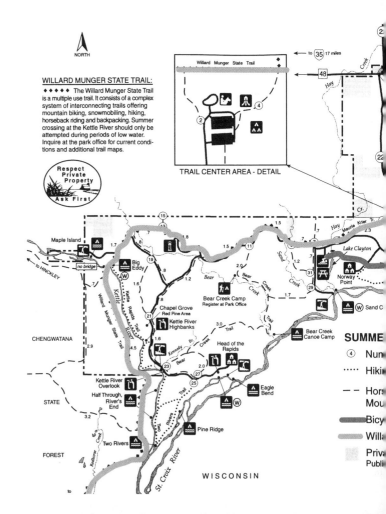

## FOR MORE INFORMATION:

St. Croix State Park
Route 3, Box 450
Hinckley, MN 55037
320-384-6591

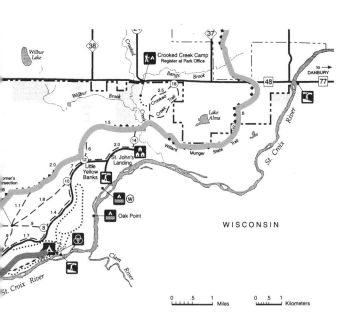

**FACILITIES**

| | |
|---|---|
| 🏛 | Park HQ / Ranger Station |
| 🎑 | Picnic Area |
| 🏠 | Overlook |
| 🗼 | Observation Tower |
| 🏛 | Trail Center |
| 🏊 | Swimming |
| 🛶 | Canoe Access |

| | |
|---|---|
| 🔺 | Campground |
| 🏠 | Group Center |
| 🔺 | Primitive Group Camp |
| 🏕 | Backpack Camping |
| 🐴 | Equestrian Area |
| ⚓ | Watercraft Camping |
| ⊛ | Interpretive Center |
| Ⓦ | Drinking Water |

**ILS**
- Gate
- Hiking/biking
- ing
- ger State Trail
- perty ohibited

**WHERE:** North Branch to Forest Lake
**LENGTH:** 15.5 miles
**SURFACE:** Paved, 10' wide
**TRAIL USE:**

**Trailhead North:** At North Branch. The trail terminates at the junction of Highway 95 and 61 with parking just south of Highway 95.

**Mid Access:** At Wyoming, where you will find parking and restrooms. Also at Stacy, adjacent to Lion Park, there is parking and restrooms available.

**Trailhead South:** At the Washington County line where it connects to the Washington County trail system (see page 65). The best place to start or finish your ride would be on Broadway in the city of Forest Lake, which is actually on the Hardwood Trail.

On this trail, you will ride through a variety of natural areas including native prairie remnants, woodlands and marsh areas. Bridges cross both a west and south branch of the Sunrise River and there are frequent opportunities for spotting wildlife and birds.

Sunrise Trail is administered by Chisago County, another example of counties developing multi-use trails on their own initiative. At the south county line it connects to the Washington County Hardwood Creek Trail. Both trails are on the same rail bed so your transition from one to the other will not be noticeable except for signage. The total of 25 miles for both trails make a nice ride.

See map page 66.

---

### *FOR MORE INFORMATION:*

Trail Office
Chisago County Park and Recreation
1356 Main St.
North Branch, MN 55056
651-674-2345

Forest Lake Chamber of Commerce
92 S. Lake St.
P.O. Box 474
Forest Lake, MN 55025
651-464-3200

**WHERE:** Forest Lake to Hugo
**LENGTH:** 9.5 miles
**SURFACE:** Paved, 10' wide
**TRAIL USE:**

**Trailhead North:** Forest Lake. Although the Hardwood Trail actually starts at the county line 1½ miles north of Forest Lake, the best place to start or end your trip is in the city where parking is available. The paved trail is one block west of Highway 61 on Broadway.

**Mid Access:** 170th Street (County Road 4)

**Trailhead South:** Hugo at County Road 8. Parking is available on city streets. There are rest rooms here, as well.

The Hardwood Creek Trail is a sister trail to the Sunrise Trail and connects directly to it on the same rail bed. Washington County has allocated funds to complete paving from Forest Lake into Hugo. Until this trail is finished call 651-430-4325 for trail status. After completion call trail office at 651-430-8368.

The Hardwood Trail was developed by Washington County with the assistance of the DNR and is administered by the county parks department. The trail goes through generally open countryside, crossing three bridges en route.

Parking and facilities will be added as funds permit and extensions to connect with the Ramsey County and St. Paul trails will come eventually.

See map page 66.

---

### FOR MORE INFORMATION:

Trail Office
Washington County Parks
1515 Keats Avenue North
Lake Elmo, MN 55042
651-430-8368

Forest Lake Chamber of Commerce
92 South Lake Street
P.O. Box 474
Forest Lake, MN 55025
651-464-3200

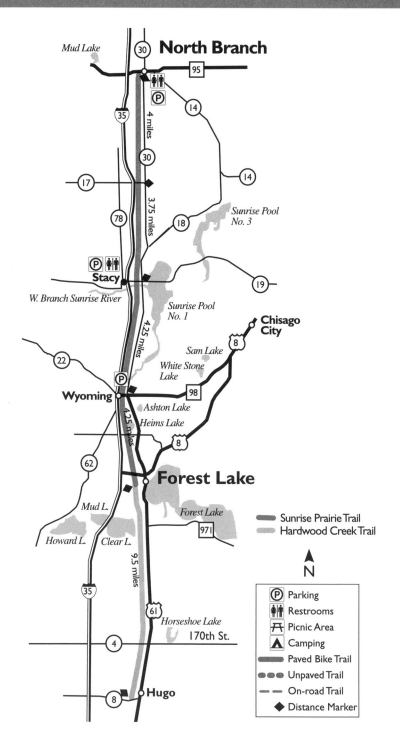

Mud Lake

**North Branch**

Sunrise Pool No. 3

W. Branch Sunrise River

Stacy

Sunrise Pool No. 1

**Chisago City**

Sam Lake

White Stone Lake

**Wyoming**

Ashton Lake

Heims Lake

**Forest Lake**

Mud L.

Forest Lake

Howard L.    Clear L.

Horseshoe Lake

170th St.

**Hugo**

Sunrise Prairie Trail
Hardwood Creek Trail

N

Ⓟ Parking
Restrooms
Picnic Area
Camping
Paved Bike Trail
Unpaved Trail
On-road Trail
◆ Distance Marker

## Trail Use Tips

Respect the rights of other trail users. Always yield to hikers, horses and other animals.

Pass with care to avoid startling other users.

Stay on trails to preserve fragile ecosystems.

Control your speed, especially on hills and around curves.

Don't litter, put in proper place.

Plan ahead for your own safety.

Drug or alcohol use is prohibited.

Camping and fires are not allowed.

Be careful of poisonous plants.

Don't feed the wild animals.

Leave wild flowers alone. Do not pick!

Never eat wild berries.

Respect privately owned land adjacent to trail.

**WHERE:** Hinckley to Carlton
**LENGTH:** 55 miles
**SURFACE:** Paved, except for 3 miles (signed) on the road shoulder south from Carlton

**TRAIL USE:**

**Trailhead South:** Exit I-35 at Hinckley and go west to old Highway 61. Turn north and continue to County Road 18, then turn west across the tracks to a parking lot with restrooms on the Grindstone River.

**Mid Access:** Since this segment closely parallels I-35, accesses at a number of towns and freeway exits are available. South to north they include Finlayson, Willow River, Sturgeon Lake, Moose Lake, Barnum and County Road 4 (Exit 227). There is a 2.2 mile paved bikeway connecting the trail to Sandstone and Banning State Park.

**Trailhead North:** At Carlton with parking and new facilities one block south of County Road 1 near downtown. It took considerable time and expense to span this former short trail interruption near this city.

We list this as a separate segment of the present 70-mile Willard Munger Trail since it is both the longest part and quite different from the Carlton-Duluth Segment. You will find a very flat rail bed with scattered forest, open farmlands, while the Carlton-Duluth portion has a steady incline and is more wooded and winding. With all segments combined, the Munger Trail is currently the longest paved trail in the world.

As you ride north of Hinckley, you are riding on the same rail bed which played a very important role during the Hinckley Forest Fire of 1894. Do plan to spend some extra time and tour the Hinckley Fire Museum near downtown. Also, within a short ride from Hinckley is the Mission Creek 1894 Theme Park and Tobies restaurant and complex on the east side of I-35.

## FOR MORE INFORMATION:

DNR Trail Office
Route 2, 701 S. Kenwood
Moose Lake, MN 55767
218-485-5410

Munger Trail Towns Association
205 Elm Avenue
P.O. Box 110
Moose Lake, MN 55767
888-263-0586

North from Barnum the trail is more sheltered and scenic including a tunnel under Highway 61. This is the most recently completed portion of this trail. Local landowner and community opposition prevented acquisition of the rail bed for quite some time after first proposed in the early 80s. Subsequent observation of the success and economic impact of the completed portions of the trail convinced all involved that bicyclists support local economies.

This is a long trail, but there are many opportunities to tour shorter portions. There are good motels in Moose Lake, Hinckley, Barnum and Carlton. An overnight will permit you to include the 14½ mile Carlton-Duluth segment and/or the Alex Laveau Trail, both of which go in and near the Jay Cooke State Park east of Carlton.

### Bike Shorts

A word about dogs, many of whom seem to take particular objection to bicycles. If you encounter one, the first requirement is not to panic. If the dog is only testing, and not actually attacking, a shout or order may keep it at bay. If it is very aggressive, the best defense is to dismount, keeping the bike between you and the dog. Grab any thing available to throw or pretend to throw. Most of all, keep moving as a dog is only going to defend what it perceives to be the limits of its territory.

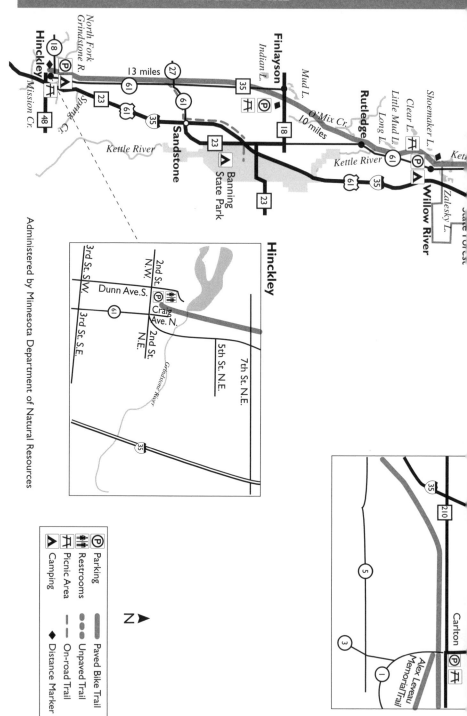

Administered by Minnesota Department of Natural Resources

**Legend:**

- Ⓟ Parking
- 🚻 Restrooms
- 🏕 Picnic Area
- ▲ Camping
- ━━━ Paved Bike Trail
- ∙∙∙ Unpaved Trail
- --- On-road Trail
- ◆ Distance Marker

N ▶

**Moose Lake by-pass**

Coffee Lake

Moosehead Lake

Echo Lake

Moose Lake State Park

**Sturgeon Lake**

Moose Horn R.
9 miles

**Moose Lake**

Sand L.

Sturgeon L.

Island L.

Moose Lake State Park

4 miles

**Barnum**

Little Hanging Horn L.

Hanging Horn L.

**Barnum**

Moose Horn River

17 miles

**Mahtowa**

Lake Twentynine

Crystal Lake

Munson Lake

Hizer Lake

Blackhoof Creek

**Atkinson**

**Otter Creek**

Little Otter Cr.

Otter Cr.

**Carlton Area Link**

**Carlton**

**Scanlon**

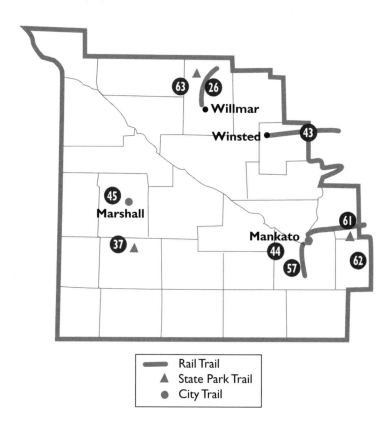

Willmar

Winsted

Marshall

Mankato

Rail Trail
State Park Trail
City Trail

## Southwest Minnesota

Trail

**\* Numbers refer to large map on page 11 and opposite page**

**WHERE:** Willmar to Hawick
**LENGTH:** 18 miles, 12 paved
**SURFACE:** Blacktop, 10' wide
**TRAIL USE:** 🚴 🚶 🛼 ➡️ 🐎

**Trailhead South:** The Willmar Civic Center 3 miles NE of downtown. Take Highway 71 and 23 north from downtown Willmar and turn east on Civic Center Road or take the bypass 71 and 23 from east Willmar to Civic Center Road. You will find ample parking and restrooms here.

**Mid Access:** At Spicer, the trail parallels Highway 23 on the west side all the way through town. You will find ample parking and restrooms here. Be careful, though, since there are a few street crossings. Future plans include moving the "Whistle Stop" depot, presently three miles out, to the intersection of the trail and County Road 10.

At New London, the trail skirts the SE edge of this charming town, with access on County Road 9 and at County Road 40 (just off 4th avenue SE).

**Trailhead North:** Across Highway 23 from Hawick is the present terminus and the northern end of the DNR improvements to date. There is parking south of Highway 23 in Hawick.

Completed in 1995, this relatively short rail-trail traverses the heart of the lake and resort area of Kandiyohi County. North of New London you will ride open vistas, but it is generally scenic with opportunities for refreshments and rest stops. You will find this trail a great initial step toward establishing some off-road and/or rail-trails in western Minnesota. Adjacent to the trail the DNR has included a separate horse riding trail between Willmar and New London which will be groomed for snowmobiling. You may occasionally encounter horseback riders.

Green Lake is truly one of the great swimming and boating lakes in Minnesota, with an excellent public swimming beach including facilities in Spicer. A stop for a swim is highly recommended — weather permitting. Consider packing fishing gear also, since there is excellent fishing at several locations along the trail.

Plan to include a street side trip through New London. Its wooded hills and several glacial ponds make a charming community. Sinclair Lewis described New London as "sitting among its ponds like a Cape Cod village." Take Main Street (Highway 9) to downtown and Birch Street back to the trail.

The DNR has acquired the abandoned trail bed as far as Richmond, and plans to extend the trail corridor all the way to St. Cloud providing some 50 miles overall. The New London to Hawick segment is crushed granite.

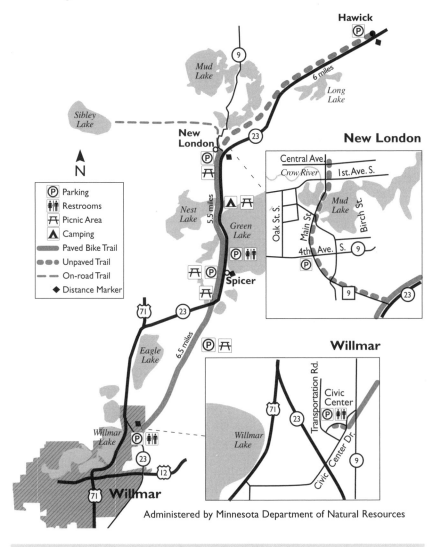

Administered by Minnesota Department of Natural Resources

### FOR MORE INFORMATION:

Trail Office
P.O. Box 508
New London, MN 56273
320-354-4940

Willmar Chamber of Commerce
2104 East Highway 12
Willmar, MN 56201
320-235-0300

**WHERE:** Currie
**LENGTH:** 6 miles
**SURFACE:** Paved
**TRAIL USE:**

**Access:** County Road 17 at Currie

The paved trail system includes 3 miles from Currie north to the park and 3 miles within the park.

This park takes you back through time. A granite monument marks the burial site of victims of the Dakota uprising of 1862. View the relocated "Koch" cabin, home of the Koch family during the Dakota Uprising. There are also four pioneer cabin sites along the interpretive trail. After a picnic overlooking Lake Shetek, hike the trail heading north to the boat ramp. From there, a self-guided interpretive trail heads out and circles Loon Island. There is another trail from the boat landing back to the picnic area and the swimming beach, which has a changing house for those wishing to cool off.

---

### FOR MORE INFORMATION:

Lake Shetek State Park
R.R.1, Box 164
Currie, MN 56123
507-763-3256

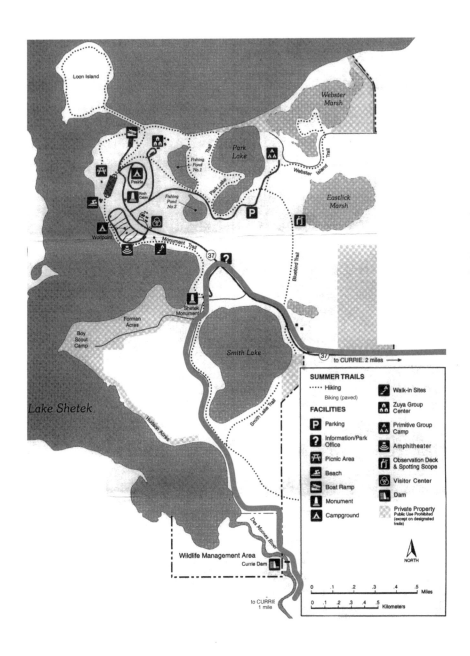

Loon Island

Webster
Marsh

Park
Lake

Fishing
Pond
No.1

Park Lake Trail

Webster Island Trail

Eastlick
Marsh

Prairie

Koch
Cabin

Fishing
Pond
No.2

P

Wolfpoint

Monument Trail

37

?

Bluebird Trail

Shetek
Monument

Forman
Acres

Boy
Scout
Camp

Smith Lake

37  to CURRIE. 2 miles ⟶

Lake Shetek

Hudson Acres

Smith Lake Trail

**SUMMER TRAILS**

Hiking

Biking (paved)

**FACILITIES**

P  Parking

?  Information/Park Office

Picnic Area

Beach

Boat Ramp

Monument

Campground

Walk-in Sites

Zuya Group Center

Primitive Group Camp

Amphitheater

Observation Deck & Spotting Scope

Visitor Center

Dam

Private Property
Public Use Prohibited
(except on designated trails)

NORTH

0  .1  .2  .3  .4  .5
Miles

0  .1  .2  .3  .4  .5
Kilometers

Des Moines River

Wildlife Management Area

Currie Dam

to CURRIE
1 mile

**WHERE:** Plymouth to Winsted
**LENGTH:** 30 miles
**SURFACE:** Crushed Limestone
**TRAIL USE:**

**Trailhead East:** From I-494, exit west on Highway 12 (Wayzata Boulevard) to County Road 15 (Gleason Lake Road). Exit and turn north on Vicksburg Lane. Continue north to 10th Avenue North (there is a sign), and turn west one-half block to the parking lot with restrooms. The City of Plymouth has paved a spur east to I-494 as part of their development of Parkers Lake. If you are traveling west on Highway 55, west of I-494, turn south at Vicksburg Lane.

**Mid Access:** Several county roads cross this trail, but the best parking is at Winsted, Silver Lake, Hutchinson and Stubbs Bay Road in Watertown.

**Trailhead West:** The limestone surface actually ends at County Road 9 in Winsted but the parking lot is a short distance east on Lake Winsted. There is a county park with facilities at the southern tip of Lake Winsted. Best parking is at the boat ramp parking lot. Parking and facilities are planned for Cedar Mills.

The Luce Line State Trail actually begins at the parking lot on 10th Avenue North just off Vicksburg Lane, but the City of Plymouth paved a short section east to I-494.

Through the foresight of the Luce Line Trail Association and subsequently the State Legislature, the right of way continues west from Plymouth for 51 miles. There has been considerable recent activity by the DNR to improve and expand this trail. Many bridges have been replaced including one to be built over the new bypass road around Hutchinson. Improvements to the trail from Winsted west to Cedar Mills will be continuing so you may want to postpone biking west of Winsted until completed. Call 320-234-7616 for current information west of Winsted. The trail is crushed rock from Wayzata west with 3 miles paved through Hutchinson and current plans include paving 14 miles from Silver Lake through Hutchinson to Cedar Mills. The balance of the trail will probably remain crushed rock for some time.

Fifty-one miles may necessitate a two vehicle outing unless you want to make it a long trip or take only a portion of the trail. Throughout most of the Plymouth to Winsted route, the rail bed is lined with trees on both sides and sometimes with cuts through thick woods. This provides a generally sheltered and cool ride. En route, you will ride through the Wayzata Country Club and past lakes and marshes. The further west you go, the more open it becomes.

Current DNR plans are to extend this trail to its full 63 miles when funds are available. Paving is probably a few years away, but bridge work and grade improvements are being done.

We prefer to start at the east end but wind direction may be a consideration. Although there are few towns, Lyndale is an interesting stop for refreshments. Be sure to bring your water bottle and have snacks in your pack for this trail.

See map page 80.

### Bike Shorts

Give an audible sound (we recommend a bike bell) before passing pedestrians or other cyclists.

### FOR MORE INFORMATION:

DNR Trail West
20596 Highway 7
Hutchinson, MN 55350
320-234-7616

Luce Line Trail Office
3980 Watertown Road
Maple Plain, MN 55359
612-475-0371

Twin West Chamber of Commerce
10550 Wayzata Blvd.
Minnetonka, MN 55343
612-540-0234

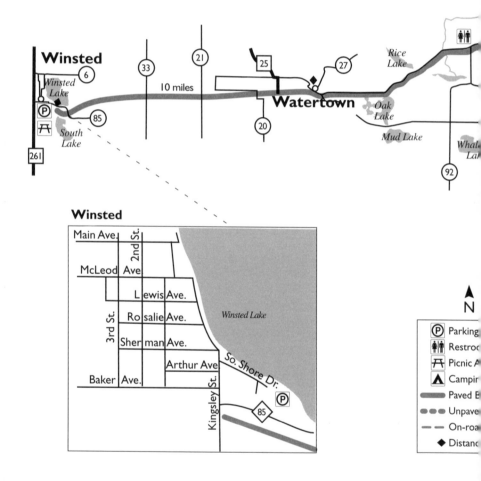

**Winsted**

Winsted Lake

South Lake

**Watertown**

10 miles

Rice Lake

Oak Lake

Mud Lake

Whal... La...

**Winsted**

Main Ave.
2nd St.
McLeod Ave
3rd St.
Lewis Ave.
Rosalie Ave.
Sherman Ave.
Arthur Ave
Baker Ave.
Kingsley St.
So. Shore Dr.
Winsted Lake

N

Parking
Restroc...
Picnic A...
Campir...
Paved B...
Unpave...
On-roa...
Distanc...

Administered by Minnesota Department of Natural Resources

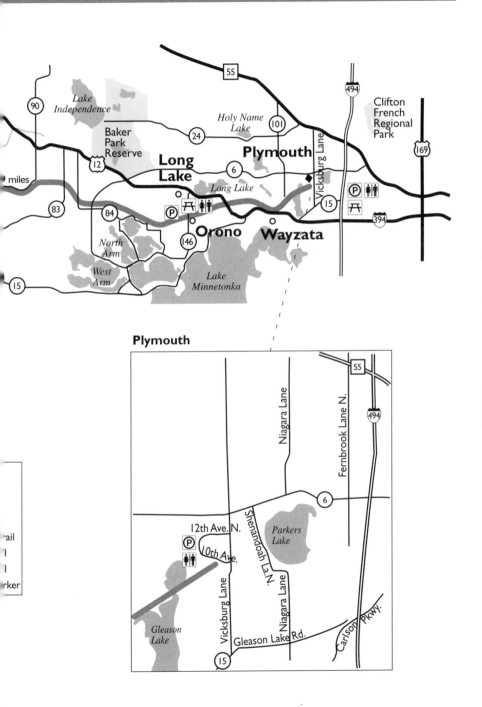

**Plymouth**

**WHERE:** City of Mankato
**LENGTH:** 7 miles
**SURFACE:** paved
**TRAIL USE:**

The City of Mankato continues to expand its network of paved off-road bike paths within the city limits. Miles of off-road trail are scattered at several locations throughout the city (see map). While connections between paved trails is mostly via street, considerable expansion is in the planning stages.

Of particular note will be construction of a connecting link between the Sakatah Trail and the downtown biking headquarters in the depot on Riverfront and Main Street. It will parallel the east bank of the Minnesota River north to Highway 14, then east to the Sakatah on Lime Valley Road. Funding has been approved for this link, but actual work suspended pending final location of an east-west railway planned for this area.

There is currently a paved off-road link from the depot to the Trailhead North of the 5½ mile Red Jacket Trail (see page 86).

Mankato has many amenities to take advantage of, including the charm of older brick buildings that were built with intricate design appendages. In the Mankato area you'll find the Mankato Civic Center, Blue Earth County Heritage Center, the Judge Lorin P. Cray Mansion, the R.D. Hubbard House, "urban" restaurants and many fun goings on. Nearly 20 parks and nearby Minneopa State Park (complete with waterfall), provide lots of area for outdoor activities. Be on the look-out for officers on bikes, which are a common sight downtown, not because of crime, but for ease of getting around and to have a closer relationship with people.

### FOR MORE INFORMATION:

Mankato Chamber and Visitors
  Bureau
122 S. Riverfront Dr.
Mankato, MN 56002
507-345-4519

Mankato Parks Department
P.O. Box 3368
Mankato, MN 56002
507-387-8650

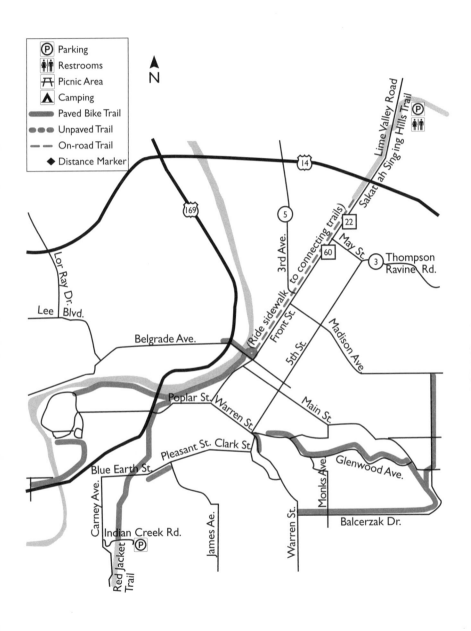

Legend:
- (P) Parking
- Restrooms
- Picnic Area
- Camping
- Paved Bike Trail
- Unpaved Trail
- On-road Trail
- ◆ Distance Marker

N

Lime Valley Road

Sakat'ah Sing'ing Hills Trail

14

169

5

3rd Ave.

22

60

May St.

3 Thompson Ravine Rd.

Lor Ray Dr.

Lee Blvd.

Ride sidewalk to connecting trails

Front St.

Madison Ave.

Belgrade Ave.

5th St.

Poplar St.

Warren St.

Main St.

Pleasant St.

Clark St.

Blue Earth St.

Glenwood Ave.

Monks Ave.

Carney Ave.

James Ae.

Warren St.

Balcerzak Dr.

Indian Creek Rd. (P)

Red Jacket Trail

**WHERE:** City of Marshall
**LENGTH:** Several miles
**SURFACE:** Paved
**TRAIL USE:** 🚴 🚶 🏕 🎿

Marshall's bike trails are not extensive, but the Country Club Drive, Highway 7 and Redwood River diversion channel route make for a great ride.

Several parks with various facilities are also located within the city, including the Marshall Aquatic Center, where you can cool off on those hot summer days, or casually stroll through the rose garden. Jeanne's Gardens, located in Independence Park, is an English garden which community volunteers maintain, creating a beautiful area of garden, landscape and wildlife habitat. Another area park is Camden State Park, just a hop, skip and jump away–10 miles south of Marshall off Highway 23.

---

### Bike Shorts

Wear an approved helmet. This is one of the most important precautions you can take to avoid serious injury.

---

*FOR MORE INFORMATION:*

Marshall CVB
P.O. Box 352B
Marshall, MN 56258
507-537-1865
www.marshall-mn.org

Marshall Parks and Recreation
344 Main St. W.
P.O. Box 477
Marshall, MN 56258
507-537-6767

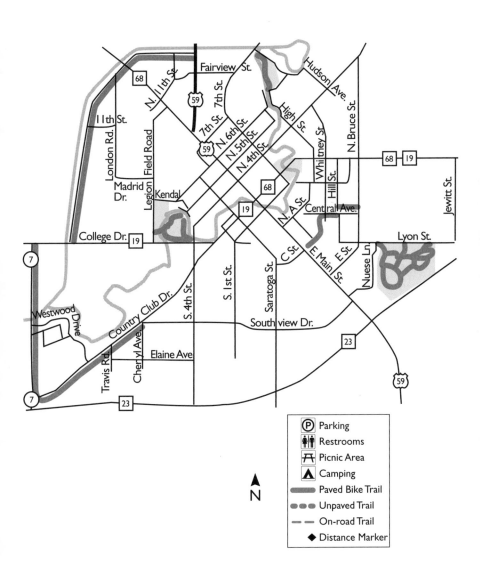

P Parking
Restrooms
Picnic Area
Camping
Paved Bike Trail
Unpaved Trail
On-road Trail
◆ Distance Marker

N

**WHERE:** Mankato to Rapidan
**LENGTH:** 5.5 miles
**SURFACE:** Paved
**TRAIL USE:**

**Trailhead North:** At the Indian Creek Road in south Mankato where it connects to a paved city bike trail. There is parking available here. Take the Front Street exit south off Highway 169. The best route to Indian Creek Road is south on Carney Avenue.

**Mid Access:** At the Red Jacket trestle crossing the Le Sueur River and State Highway 66. There is parking available on east side.

**Trailhead South:** At the Village of Rapidan, with a paved shoulder continuing west along Highway 9 to the dam on the Blue Earth River.

Although short in length, this is a great two-way ride and can be extended several miles further by utilizing the paved Mankato city off-street trails with which it connects or on paved shoulders along Highway 9, 60 and 69.

You will cross open farm country as well as views of scenic woods and river breaks along the Blue Earth River. Of special note is the Red Jacket trestle where you cross the river. This trestle is the reason why the trail exists and it is a classic. Foresighted individuals from Mankato, and especially Mr. Al Frosberg, thought the trestle worth saving and proceeded to do so. Their effort expanded into a bike trail which is the first rail-trail in Minnesota recovered for public use after years of private ownership by several landowners. This trail was constructed and is administered by Blue Earth County.

The trail includes an interesting tunnel under Highway 66 and an alternate trail adjacent to the main trail for a short distance to take you down to a parking area and across a new bridge over the Le Sueur River before re-connecting with the main trail.

### FOR MORE INFORMATION:

Blue Earth County Park Department
35 Map Drive
P.O. Box 3083
Mankato, MN 56002
507-625-3281

Mankato Chamber of Commerce
112 River Front Drive
P.O. Box 999
507-345-4519

## Mankato

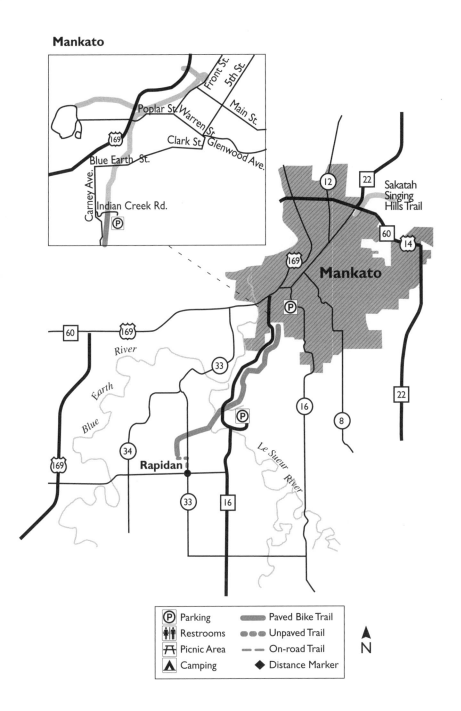

**Legend:**

- P Parking
- Restrooms
- Picnic Area
- Camping
- Paved Bike Trail
- Unpaved Trail
- On-road Trail
- ◆ Distance Marker

N

**WHERE:** Faribault to Mankato
**LENGTH:** 39 miles
**SURFACE:** Paved
**TRAIL USE:** 🚴 🚶 📷 🎿

**Trailhead East:** At West Central Faribault, near Highway 21. Parking is available 400 feet northwest of the junction at Highway 21 and the 7th Street stoplight. The trail follows old rail bed west from just south of this parking lot.

**Mid Access:** Mileages are west to east. At mile 4½ near Eagle Lake, there is parking, but no facilities. At mile 11, off County Road 26, there is parking, but no facilities. At mile 16, Elysian, there is a parking lot with a new building and restrooms. At mile 24, Waterville, just north of Highway 13 & 60 intersection, there is street parking. At mile 25, Sakatah State Park on Cannon Lake, there is parking, picnic tables, restrooms and fresh water. At mile 35, Shager County Park on Cannon Lake, there are picnic tables, parking, shelter, restrooms and fresh water.

**Trailhead West:** At Mankato, just north of Highway 14 and west of Highway 22, where it ties into the Mankato City bikeway system. Parking is one-quarter mile north of Highway 14 and 22 interchange on Lime Valley Road. There are portable toilets one-quarter mile east of lot along the trail.

A newly paved trail, Sakatah Singing Hills traverses parts of three counties along its 39 miles. This level trail wanders near lush pastures and farmland, along several lakes, through three small towns and a forested state park. There are swimming beaches within a short ride off the trail at Sakatah Lake State Park, Waterville, Elysian, Madison Lake and Cannon Lake. The fish hatchery in Waterville is open to visitors.

---

### FOR MORE INFORMATION:

Trail Office
Box 11
Elysian, MN 56028
507-267-4774

Faribault Chamber of Commerce
530 Wilson Avenue
P.O. Box 434
Faribault, MN 55021
507-334-4381

Mankato Chamber of Commerce
112 River Front Drive
P.O. Box 999
Mankato, MN 56002
507-345-4519

The proposed Mankato connection between the Sakatah trail and the city trails at the downtown depot has not been finished and is currently on hold pending possible railroad relocation in Mankato.

The trail follows city streets through the town of Waterville, but you will find it well marked and on light traffic roads. Along with the completion of paved surfacing, the DNR has improved facilities and parking availability all along this trail. You will also find an occasional picnic table at interim points along your route.

Thirty-nine miles makes a pretty good one day ride so you may want to leave a car at Faribault if the wind is westerly, or at Mankato if the wind is easterly.

If you are campers as well as bikers, Sakatah State Park is 15 miles from the Faribault trailhead. In our group opinion, the east 14 miles is the most scenic as well as the most shaded and would make an excellent two-way ride.

One should consider the lakeside town of Elysian as a starting point for both portions of the trail. It is very near the half-way point and has an excellent parking lot and shelter with restrooms and water.

Located on the banks of the Minnesota River, Mankato is the home of Mankato State University. Minneopa Falls in Minneopa State Park is 5 miles west on Highway 68 and US 169.

## Mankato

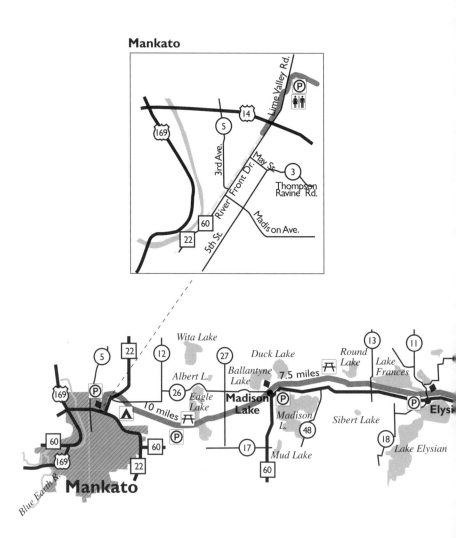

Administered by Minnesota Department of Natural Resources

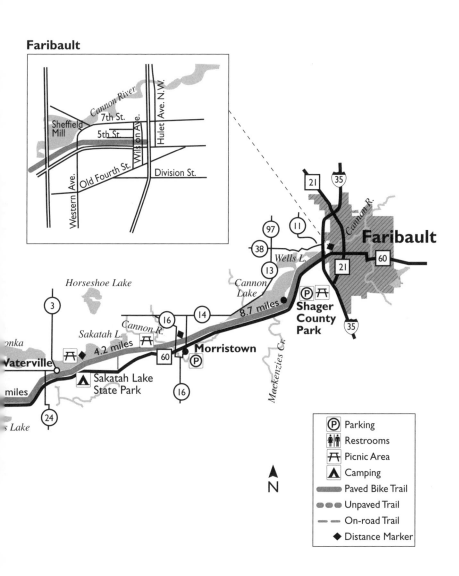

**Faribault**

Cannon River
7th St.
Sheffield Mill
5th St.
Western Ave.
Old Fourth St.
Wilson Ave.
Hulet Ave. N.W.
Division St.

21
35
Faribault
97
11
38
Wells L.
13
60
21
Horseshoe Lake
Cannon Lake
8.7 miles
3
P  A
Shager County Park
35
Cannon R.
16
14
Sakatah L.
Cannon R.
onka
4.2 miles
60
Morristown
P
Waterville
P
A  Sakatah Lake State Park
Mackenzies Cr.
miles
16
24
s Lake

N

| | |
|---|---|
| P | Parking |
| 🚻 | Restrooms |
| A | Picnic Area |
| A | Camping |
| ▬ | Paved Bike Trail |
| ●●● | Unpaved Trail |
| – – | On-road Trail |
| ◆ | Distance Marker |

# SAKATAH STATE PARK

**WHERE:** Waterville
**LENGTH:** 3 mile portion of Sakatah Singing Hills State Trail traverses through the center of this park
**SURFACE:** Paved
**TRAIL USE:** 🚴 🚶 🚻 🎿

**Access:** Park entrance is on Highway 60, east of Waterville.

Sakatah State Park is located on the east edge of Waterville and provides excellent camping and hiking. Biking is pretty much limited to the state trail but restroom facilities are available just off the trail.

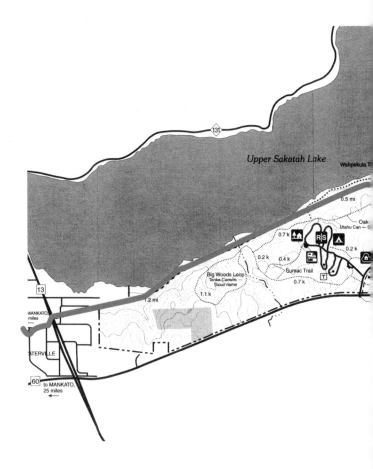

## FOR MORE INFORMATION:

Sakatah Lake State Park
R.R.2, Box 19
Waterville, MN 56096
507-362-4438

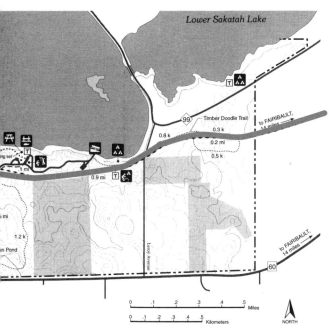

Lower Sakatah Lake

**TRAILS**
······· Hiking Only
········· Hiking/Ski
– – – Snowmobile
‑ ‑ ‑ Sakatah Singing Hills Trail
   • Snowmobiling
   • Skiing
   • Hiking
   • Bicycling

**FACILITIES**
❓ Information/Office
🏕 Picnic Area
◎ Interpretive/Trail Center
🎣 Fishing Pier
⛵ Boat Ramp
▲ Campground
🔼 Primitive Group Camp

🚴 Bicycle Touring Camp
🚉 Trailer Sanitation Station
🔼🔼 Camper Cabin
🏐 Volleyball Court
R|S Restrooms/Showers
⬜ Private Property
Public Use Prohibited
(except on designated trails)
T Toilets

**WHERE:** Willmar/New London
**LENGTH:** 5 miles
**SURFACE:** Paved
**TRAIL USE:** 🚲 🚶 🛷 ➜ ⛷ 🐴

**Access:** 15 miles north of Willmar on US Highway 48.

Although part of this trail goes along the shore of Lake Andrew, expect some hills elsewhere.

---

### Bike Shorts

Plan your ride so you are off the streets, roads and trails by dusk. Bicycles are best left parked or stored at night, but if you must, be sure you have front, side and rear reflectors, plus lights. Wear or switch to light-colored clothing.

Adults today are very health conscious and bicycling is one of the best forms of exercise. In addition to fitness and family fun, rail-trails provide an important contribution to regional economies.

---

### *FOR MORE INFORMATION:*

Sibley State Park
800 Sibley Park Road N.E.
New London, MN 56273
320-354-2055

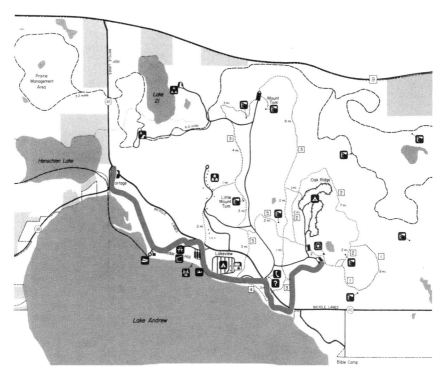

**LEGEND**

**TRAILS**

............ Hiking

– – – Horseback / Hiking

–··–··– Bicycle / Interpretive

――― Canoe Route

**TRAIL NAMES**

1 Pondview

2 Parker - Fremberg

3 Mount Tom

4 Lakeview

5 Oak Hills

PRIVATE PROPERTY
Public Use Prohibited
(except on designated trails)

**FACILITIES**

? Information / Office

Picnic Area

Swimming

Boat Ramp

Overlook

Interpretive / Trail Center

Shelter

Telephone

Equestrian Area

Campground

Group Center

Primitive Group Camp

Trailer Sanitation Station

P Parking

Fishing Pier

SCALE

MILES
0 .1 .2 .3 .4 .5 1.0

KILOMETERS
0 .5 1.0 1.5

Red Wing
10
22 Cannon Falls
61 Faribault
19
Owatonna
54 59
Rochester Winona
75
60
28 Lanesboro

Rail Trail
▲ State Park Trail
• City Trail

## Southeast Minnesota

Trail

**\* Numbers refer to large map on page 11 and opposite page**

**WHERE:** Cannon Falls to Red Wing
**LENGTH:** 19.7 miles
**SURFACE:** Blacktop
**TRAIL USE:** 🚲 🚶 🏕 🎿

**Trailhead West:** Cannon Falls–Exit Highway 52 on County Road 19 into Cannon Falls. Parking lot is on Highway 19 one block west of Main Street.

**Mid Access:** Highway 19 east from Cannon Falls to County Road 7, north to Welch. Or, Highway 61 east of Miesville to County Road 7 south. There is parking, shelter, picnic tables, restrooms and water here.

**Trailhead East:** Old West Main Street and Bench Street, one block off Highway 61 in west Red Wing. There is a parking lot with facilities. To downtown Red Wing, you may follow Old West Main along the marked historic route near the Mississippi River.

For a trail with great scenery in all seasons, shelter from the wind and shade from the hot sun, this is the place to be. The trail follows the Cannon River Valley from Cannon Falls to Red Wing. At 19.7 miles, it is a short one-way ride or a quite manageable two-way trip. Although not part of the DNR State Trail system, this is a scenic, well-maintained, paved trail. A daily or seasonal "wheelpass" is required for trail use. This trail suffered some flood damage in 1998, but the trail is open and funds are on hand for permanent repairs.

"Wheelpasses" are for users 18 years or older, and refer to anything with wheels: bicycles, in-line skates, skateboards, etc. They are available at self-purchasing stations at major access points, from merchants in Cannon Falls and Red Wing, or you may encounter an attendant along the trail.

For this gem of a trail, we are indebted to a group of private citizens from Cannon Falls, Welch and Red Wing who saw the recreational value of the area. They secured the property and obtained the grants and assistance to improve it and replace the numerous bridges you will cross. The trail parallels the river along the south side between bluffs and trees with few stretches of open country. The many bridges tell the rider there are a lot of small gorges and feeder steams which empty into the Cannon River.

If you plan to ride both ways on your day, we recommend starting at Red Wing, where there is a parking lot near the beginning of the trail just off old West Main Street. This gives you an opportunity to explore

Red Wing with its old river-town flavor. It also gives you the benefit of the slight downhill grade on the last one-half of the trip, rather than the first half. Along the way, you will find picnic tables about 3½ miles east of Cannon Falls, and portable restrooms at approximately one-third distance intervals. Refreshments in the village of Welch are available if you wish to take a short side trip.

Some local sites in the area include the beautifully restored St. James Hotel in Red Wing, where you also might consider a Mississippi River cruise. Cannon Falls offers canoeing and tubing on the Cannon River.

See map page 100.

*Cannon Valley Trail sign*

### FOR MORE INFORMATION:

Trail Office
306 West Mill St.
Cannon Falls, MN 55009
507-263-0508

Cannon Falls Chamber of Commerce
103 N. 4th St.
P.O. Box 2
Cannon Falls, MN 55009
507-263-2289

Red Wing Area
 Chamber of Commerce
420 Levee Street
Red Wing, MN 55066
651-388-4719

**Cannon Falls**

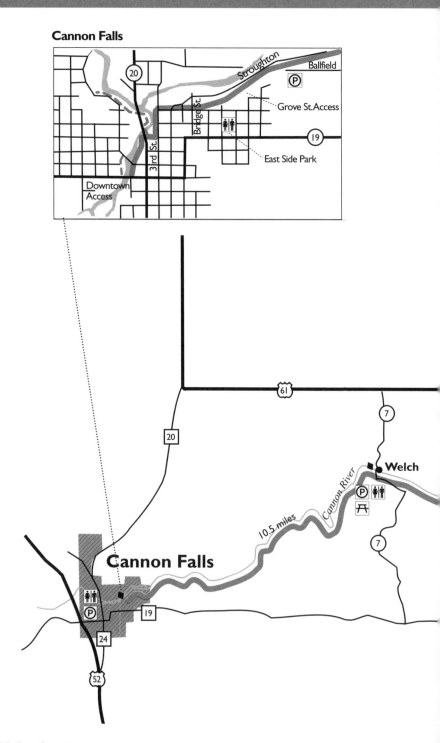

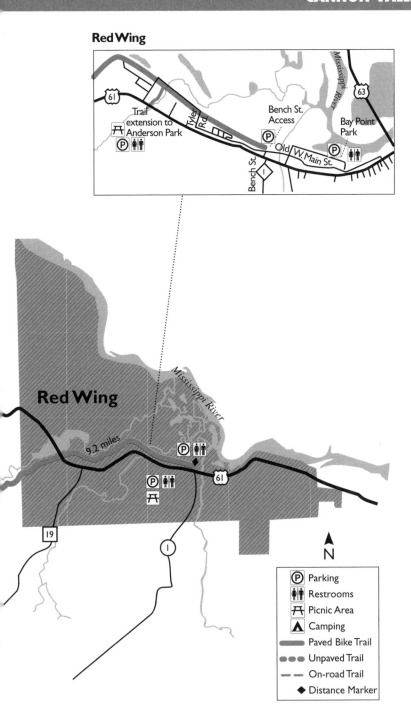

**Red Wing**

Bench St. Access

Bay Point Park

Trail extension to Anderson Park

Red Wing

9.2 miles

Legend:
- P Parking
- Restrooms
- Picnic Area
- Camping
- Paved Bike Trail
- Unpaved Trail
- On-road Trail
- Distance Marker

N

**WHERE:** Pine Island to Rochester
**LENGTH:** 12.5 miles
**SURFACE:** Blacktop
**TRAIL USE:**

**Trailhead North:** Pine Island Park on the NE corner of Pine Island just south of exit from Highway 52. You will find parking, restrooms, water and picnic tables here.

**Mid Access:** Douglas on County Road 14, exit off highway 52. There is a large parking lot, shelter, water and restrooms at milepost 5 from Rochester.

**Trailhead South:** About 2 miles NW of Rochester on County Road 4, or, if you are driving on Highway 52, take the IBM exit west to County Road 4. There is ample paved parking, shelter and portable restrooms here.

The Douglas Trail is one of the few in the state that can be covered in its entirety, riding both directions, in less than four hours. Its 12½ mile length combined with easy access and adequate parking at both trailheads make this an excellent half-day, one-vehicle trip. Repair and widening of some bad spots have been done with complete widening and resurfacing planned. Benches, tables and a shelter have recently been added along the trail.

This is a good choice for an early or late season ride when that unusually nice day comes along, but we recommend it at any time during the biking season.

En route, you will cross the Zumbro River and Plum Creek on wide, refurbished bridges. The trail itself is wide and in excellent condition, with the only hazard being the need to cross several country gravel roads. The trail winds past a golf course and through fertile farm country. It is not heavily wooded, but there is tree cover much of the way. You may encounter horseback riders as a horse and cross-country ski trail parallel the bike path and the two cross at occasional well-marked points.

Following the recent construction of the Circle Drive road around north and west Rochester, two bike path overpasses have been added. One crosses 41st St. N.W. and one crosses Circle Drive near the golf course. Access to parts of the Rochester City Trail system (page 109) is available at both sites. Rochester has many areas of interest, including the Mayo Clinic and Museum, Mayowood, and the 30,000 giant Canada geese that live at Silver Lake Park. Bring a bag of bread and wear shoes.

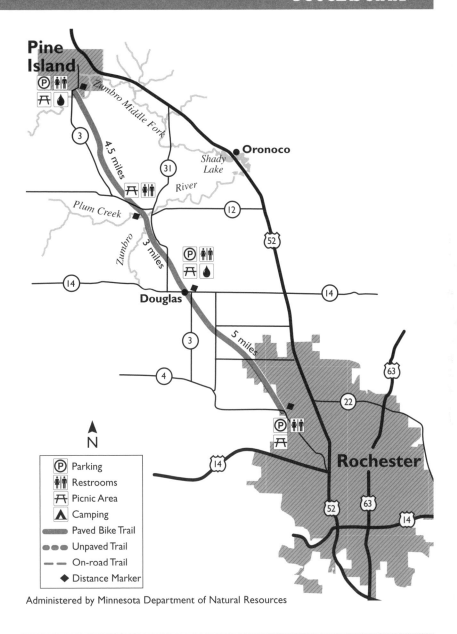

**Pine Island**

Zumbro Middle Fork

3

4.5 miles

31

Shady Lake

**Oronoco**

River

Plum Creek

12

52

Zumbro

3 miles

14

14

**Douglas**

3

5 miles

4

63

22

N

**Rochester**

14

52

63

14

- Ⓟ Parking
- Restrooms
- Picnic Area
- ▲ Camping
- ▬ Paved Bike Trail
- ●●● Unpaved Trail
- - - On-road Trail
- ◆ Distance Marker

Administered by Minnesota Department of Natural Resources

## FOR MORE INFORMATION:

Rochester Visitor Bureau
150 South Broadway Suite A
Rochester, MN 55904
507-288-4331
800-634-8277

Trail Office
2300 Silver Creek Road N.E.
Rochester, MN 55906
507-285-7176

**WHERE:** City of Faribault
**LENGTH:** 4 miles
**SURFACE:** Paved
**TRAIL USE:**

Faribault is located at the east end of Sakatah Singing Hills State Trail, which gives it a direct connection to Mankato 39 miles to the west. The planned connection to Faribault's city trails has not yet been completed. Their paved trail following the Straight River from the north edge of town to the south edge is well worth the time.

The Mill Towns Trail is a paved recreational trail in the works that would link the Cannon Valley Trail (Cannon Falls to Red Wing) and the Sakatah Singing Hills Trail (Faribault to Mankato). This trail will skirt west and north edge of Faribault. Call Northfield Chamber of Commerce (1-507-645-5604) for updated information.

---

### Bike Shorts

Keep your tires inflated to the pressure noted on the side of the tire.

---

### *FOR MORE INFORMATION:*

Faribault Area Chamber of
  Commerce
530 Wilson Ave. N.W.
Faribault, MN 55021
507-334-4381

Parks and Recreation
15 West Division St.
City Hall
Faribault, MN 55021
507-332-6112

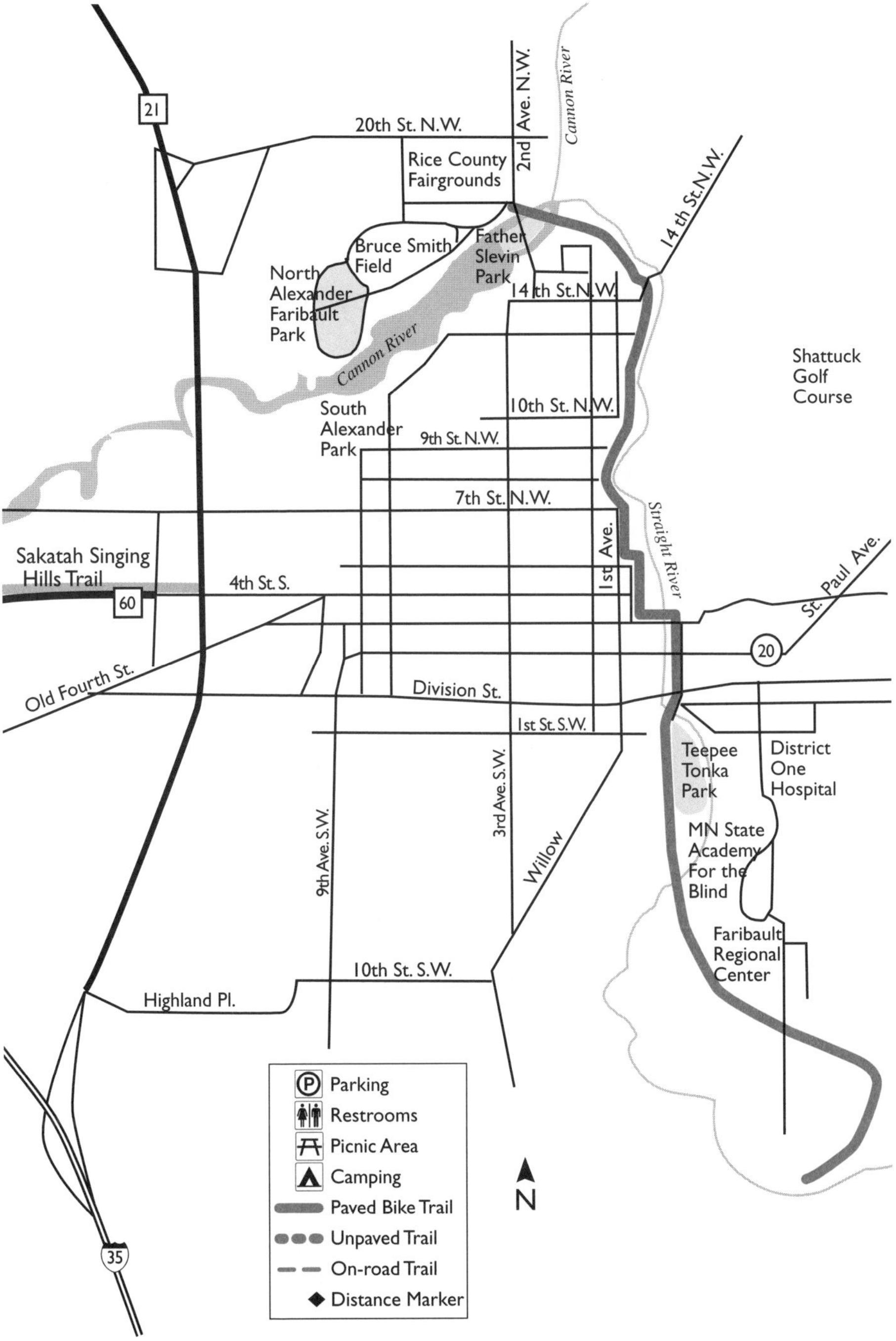
21
20th St. N.W.
2nd Ave. N.W.
Cannon River
Rice County Fairgrounds
14 th St. N.W.
Bruce Smith Field
Father Slevin Park
North Alexander Faribault Park
14 th St. N.W.
Cannon River
Shattuck Golf Course
10th St. N.W.
South Alexander Park
9th St. N.W.
7th St. N.W.
Straight River
Sakatah Singing Hills Trail
1st Ave.
St. Paul Ave.
4th St. S.
60
20
Old Fourth St.
Division St.
1st St. S.W.
Teepee Tonka Park
District One Hospital
3rd Ave. S.W.
MN State Academy For the Blind
9th Ave. S.W.
Willow
Faribault Regional Center
10th St. S.W.
Highland Pl.
Parking
Restrooms
Picnic Area
Camping
Paved Bike Trail
Unpaved Trail
On-road Trail
Distance Marker
N
35

**WHERE:** City of Owatonna
**LENGTH:** 5.75 miles
**SURFACE:** Paved, 12 feet wide
**TRAIL USE:** 🚴 🚶 🛼 ⛷️

The Owatonna trail system has been the beneficiary of four substantial contributions by estate or trusts of four entrepreneurial families. Those contributions have resulted in an exceptional trail system traversing the scenic city north to south and east to west.

The total trail system connects three major parks plus the 225 acre Kaplan Woods Parkway. All of the trail is lighted for night recreation use.

*Owatonna City Trail*

## FOR MORE INFORMATION:

Parks and Recreation Department
540 West Hill Circle
Owatonna, MN 55060
507-444-4321

Visitors Bureau and Chamber of
Commerce
507-451-7970

Owatonna CVB
320 Hoffman Drive
Owatonna, MN 55060
507-451-7970
1-800-423-6466
www.owatonna.org

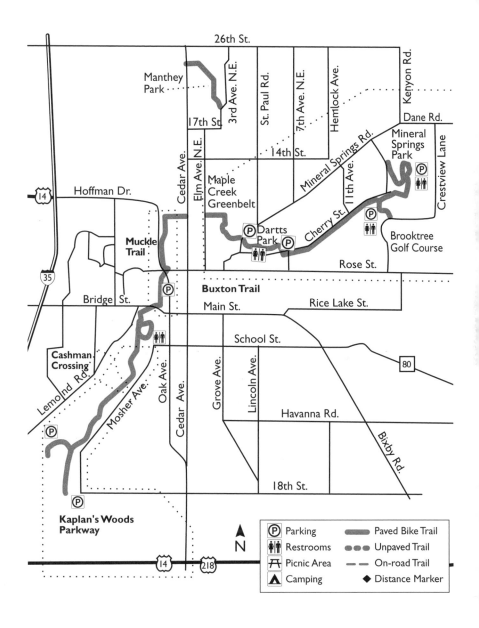

26th St.

Manthey Park

17th St

3rd Ave. N.E.

St. Paul Rd.

7th Ave. N.E.

Hemlock Ave.

Kenyon Rd.

Dane Rd.

Mineral Springs Park

Crestview Lane

14th St.

Mineral Springs Rd.

11th Ave.

Cherry St.

Cedar Ave.

Elm Ave. N.E.

Maple Creek Greenbelt

Hoffman Dr.

14

Muckle Trail

Dartts Park

Brooktree Golf Course

Rose St.

Buxton Trail

Bridge St.

Main St.

Rice Lake St.

School St.

Cashman Crossing

Lemond Rd.

Mosher Ave.

Oak Ave.

Cedar Ave.

Grove Ave.

Lincoln Ave.

Havanna Rd.

80

Bixby Rd.

18th St.

Kaplan's Woods Parkway

35

**N**

| | | |
|---|---|---|
| Ⓟ Parking | | ▬▬ Paved Bike Trail |
| Restrooms | | ●●● Unpaved Trail |
| ⊼ Picnic Area | | ― ― On-road Trail |
| ▲ Camping | | ◆ Distance Marker |

14    218

## ROCHESTER (CITY)

**WHERE:** City of Rochester
**LENGTH:** 26 miles
**SURFACE:** Paved
**TRAIL USE:** 

Rochester has a number of parks with good trails, as well as off-road trails following the Zumbro River and a new connection to the Douglas State Trail northwest of the city. Their routes and paths are well-marked and quite extensive.

## FOR MORE INFORMATION:

Rochester CVB
150 So. Broadway, Suite A
Rochester, MN 55904
507-288-4331, 1-800-634-8277
www.rochestercvb.org

Rochester Parks
201-4th St. S.E.
Rochester, MN 55904
507-281-6160

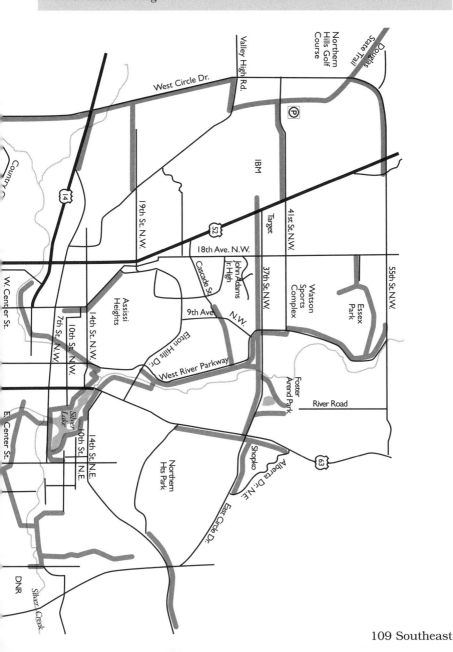

**WHERE:** Fountain to Houston
**LENGTH:** 42 miles
**SURFACE:** Paved
**TRAIL USE:**

**Trailhead West:** At the South end of the Main St. in Fountain. There is parking, as well as rest rooms here.

**Mid Access:** At Whalen, where you will find restrooms and picnic tables. At Lanesboro, the trail passes through the center of town, crossing County Road 250.

There is also access at the Isinours Unit on County Road 17. The parking lot is located about one-quarter mile west of County Road 17 at the Isinours wood lot. This is also the Trailhead North of the Harmony-Preston Valley Trail (see page 113).

**Trailhead East:** Houston, a new trail center building at 200 West Plum Street where information, full facilities and parking are available.

The Root River Trail now provides 42 paved miles along the Root River Valley and through the hardwood forest and bluffs of this historic region. Consider it for an early or late season ride, but it is great any time of the year. It is one of the more level trails except at the extreme west end and a short adjustment about mid-point between Fountain and Lanesboro.

Trail Headquarters: At the former depot in Rushford, located one block west of Mill Street (which is also Highway 43) and adjacent to the downtown area. The depot is open year-round and is being developed into a railroad and trail museum.

The 42 miles make this a fairly long one-way ride for the casual bicyclist, but the opportunities and attractions of this general area suggest an overnight stay at one of the several bed and breakfasts or motels along or near it.

The Root River State Trail follows the watershed and general route of the south branch of its namesake between Fountain and Lanesboro and joins the main branch just east of Lanesboro. Although the trail is not always adjacent to the river, you will often see trout fishermen, canoeists and other outdoor enthusiasts on your ride. The trail includes 46 bridges with lengths of up to 500 ft. Of course, the towns of Fountain, Lanesboro and Rushford are attractions in themselves, with the entire downtown section of Lanesboro listed on the National Register of Historic Places.

The route will take you through the scenic bluffs and extensive hardwood forest of southern Minnesota. Be alert for wildlife, especially through Lost Lake Game Refuge just west of Lanesboro. Worthwhile side trips include the State Fish Hatchery south of Lanesboro on Highway 16 or the Amish Community and shops at Harmony. Root River Trail towns annually sponsor a bike ride the third week in May called Sykkle Tur.

We prefer to plan this trip for a one-way ride from the Trailhead West at Fountain to Rushford and eventually Houston. The main reason is that it gives you a downhill ride all the way with one exception when the trail leaves the valley to get on top of the bluffs and returns to the rail bed after a short distance.

If your party has chosen a one-way ride, your best bet is to park a vehicle in Fountain and one in Houston. Take Highway 8 from Fountain to Lanesboro and Highway 16 from Lanesboro to Houston.

At Fountain, there is ample parking, a shelter and portable restrooms. From this point, the trail takes an immediate downhill grade for nearly two miles until it reaches the river valley. Three miles further along you will see an old railroad building and another parking lot. This was once the point where the railroad used to put on a second engine to pull the trains up the grade you just came down. It is also the site of the Isinours Demonstration Woodland, where you may want to take a walking side trip and view the many varieties of trees (labeled) with which the foresters are experimenting or are observing.

In Lanesboro you will ride by the dam which provides electricity. Lanesboro has recently constructed a new building along the trail housing both a trail office and the Lanesboro Visitor's Center, including restrooms.

Lanesboro is a picturesque village with antique shops, a winery, campground, a historic inn and bed and breakfast inns. An eatery on the Main St. has live music and wonderful food. There is a resident woodcarver and Amish gift shop, along with many other interesting attractions and eateries.

Heading east, your next stop might be Whalen where they conveniently provide picnic tables and restrooms at trailside. Your next chance for refreshments is Peterson, 9 miles further east. Nearing Rushford is the only part of the trip in open country or paralleling a highway. Once in Rushford, you will find ample parking near the depot, excellent restaurants and accommodations. Since the trail now continues beyond Rushford, you will need to traverse city streets from the Depot to pick up the paved trail on the east side of town. We recommend a route from the depot around and behind the IGA grocery store as the most direct.

See page 114 for map.

*Root River Trail*

---

**FOR MORE INFORMATION:**

Trail Office
Box 376
Lanesboro, MN 55949
507-467-2552

Lanesboro Visitor Center
100 Milwaukee Road
P.O. Box 348
Lanesboro, MN 55948
800-944-2670

**WHERE:** Harmony to Root River State Trail via Preston
**LENGTH:** 17.8 miles
**SURFACE:** Paved 10 feet wide
**TRAIL USE:**

**Trailhead North:** Isinours demonstration woodlot, just west of County Road 17 intersection with Root River State Trail. Follow County Road 8 east out of Fountain approximately 4 miles, then south 3 miles on County Road 17. You will find parking here.

**Mid Access:** Preston. One-half mile south of Highway 52 in east Preston adjacent to the fairgrounds. There is ample parking and a trail headquarters building with restrooms and information.

**Trailhead South:** Harmony on Highway 52 at 4th Street. Parking one-half mile west of Highway 52 with facilities.

A welcome link to one of the most popular trails in the state and one that provides additional bicycle access to the scenic southeastern blufflands. It crosses sparkling trout streams and views range from limestone bluffs to rolling pastoral landscapes. The north half from Preston to the Root River Trail (see page 110) is both level and scenic, while the Preston to Harmony half presents an uphill climb for part of the 12 miles, but an easy ride going north.

Preston has developed a beautiful parking area and trail building, along with many small town facilities and points of interest. The Amish community of Harmony is unique in the offering of Amish crafts and produce shops you will not find elsewhere.

### *FOR MORE INFORMATION:*

Trail Office
Box 376
Lanesboro, MN 55949
507-467-2552

Historic Bluff Country
P.O. Box 609
15-2nd St. N.W.
Harmony, MN 55939
507-886-2230
800-428-2030
FAX 507-886-2934
www.bluffcountry.com

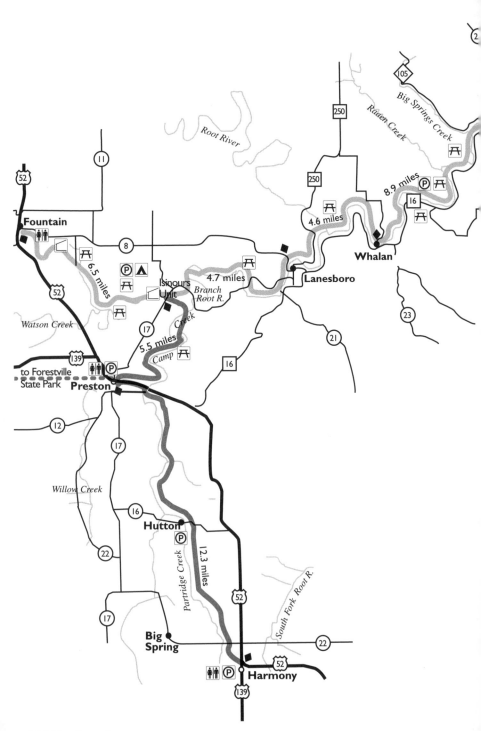

Root River

Big Springs Creek

Raven Creek

8.9 miles

4.6 miles

Whalan

Lanesboro

Fountain

6.5 miles

Branch
Root R.

4.7 miles

Isinours
Unit

Creek

Watson Creek

5.5 miles

Camp

to Forestville
State Park    Preston

Willow Creek

Hutton

12.3 miles

Partridge Creek

South Fork Root R.

Big
Spring

Harmony

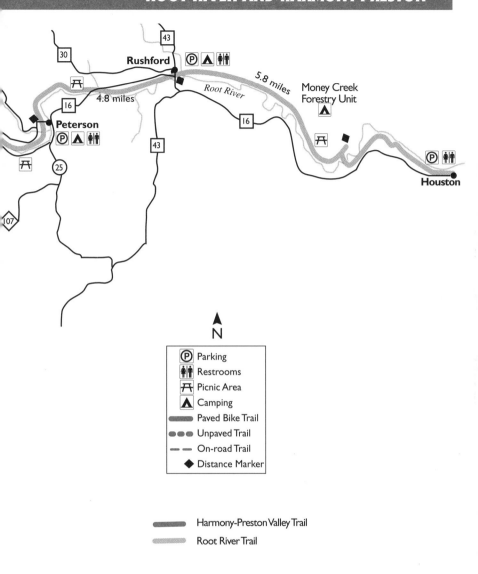

30

43

**Rushford** Ⓟ ▲ �

5.8 miles

Money Creek
Forestry Unit ▲

*Root River*

4.8 miles

16

16

**Peterson**
Ⓟ ▲ �

Ⓟ �

43

**Houston**

25

107

**N**

| | |
|---|---|
| Ⓟ | Parking |
| � | Restrooms |
| ⊼ | Picnic Area |
| ▲ | Camping |
| ▬▬ | Paved Bike Trail |
| ●●● | Unpaved Trail |
| – – | On-road Trail |
| ◆ | Distance Marker |

▬▬ Harmony-Preston Valley Trail
▬▬ Root River Trail

Administered by Minnesota Department of Natural Resources

**WHERE:** City of Winona
**LENGTH:** 5.5 miles
**SURFACE:** Paved
**TRAIL USE:** 🚴 🚶 📷 🚣

The city's primary bike trail is a circle route around Lake Winona. Plans are currently underway to construct a bicycle/hiking path on top of their extensive flood dike system. If and when it is finished, it will add several miles of off-road trail.

In addition, most of the required $691,000 cost of a new trail has been raised. The trail will connect the downtown area with the Knopp sub-division on the west near St. Mary's. An underpass under Highway 14 and also under Highway 61 are required to provide a safe bike-hike connection. It is anticipated that work will commence in 1999.

If you want a longer ride, Winona is just a few miles from the Root River Trail (see page 110) and Wisconsin's Great River Trail (see page 212).

This historic area (many buildings on National Register of Historic Places) provides lots of things to do and see while you're in Winona, complete with magnificent views of the river valley.

---

### Bike Shorts

Go with the traffic flow, signal your turns and lane changes and be especially alert for pedestrians or car doors opening when passing a line of parked cars or other roadside obstructions. Stay as close to the right side of the road as possible.

---

### FOR MORE INFORMATION:

Winona CVB
67 Main Street
Winona, MN 55987-0870
507-452-2272
1-800-657-4972
www.visitwinona.com

Winona Park and Recreation
207 Lafayette
P.O. Box 378
Winona, MN 55987

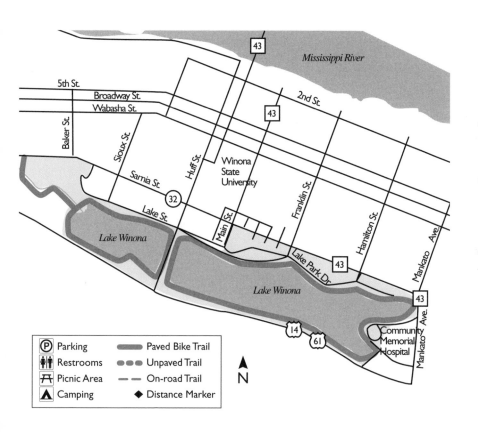

Mississippi River

5th St.
Broadway St.
Wabasha St.
2nd St.
Baker St.
Sioux St.
Sarnia St.
Huff St.
Winona State University
Franklin St.
Hamilton St.
Mankato Ave.
Lake St.
Lake Winona
Main St.
Lake Park Dr.
Lake Winona
Community Memorial Hospital
43
43
43
43
43
32
14
61

**P** Parking
**Restrooms**
**Picnic Area**
**Camping**

Paved Bike Trail
Unpaved Trail
On-road Trail
Distance Marker

N

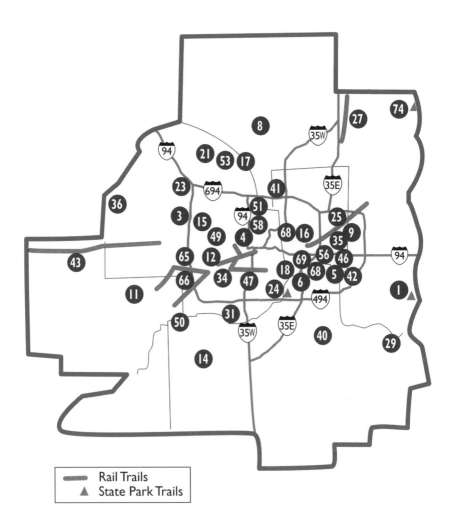

Rail Trails
▲ State Park Trails

# Metro Minnesota
## Trail

**\* Numbers refer to large map on page 11 and opposite page**

## URBAN BIKE TRAILS

Bicycling continues to grow in popularity with most communities recognizing the need to plan for safe bicycle routes. There are miles of urban bicycle paths in Minnesota, with many now under construction or in the planning stages. The emphasis in this book is on trails and paths separate from the auto roads, although many on-street lanes are included.

Consider taking the precaution of registering your bicycle with the State of Minnesota. It costs $10.00 for three years. Stickers can be purchased at some local bike shops, Hennepin County Service Centers or at a bike registration office at the Sears store on Rice Street in St. Paul.

Some metro suburbs may not be included in this section because information was either not provided, or designated bicycle paths are minimal or non-existent.

## MINNEAPOLIS AND ST. PAUL METRO TRAILS

Included in this section are several bike trails in a variety of locations across the metro area. In addition to providing trails for recreation, both cities, along with their respective park boards, continue to expand the cities' commuter bike trails and encourage this efficient means of transportation by providing numerous bicycle racks and lockers that accomodate your entire bicycle. While Minneapolis has miles of well-marked, on-street bike lanes, St. Paul has not yet developed comparable commuter bicycle routes.

In Minneapolis, bicycles are now banned from Nicollet Mall weekdays from 6AM to 6PM but the city has added new lanes and striping on alternate downtown routes on both Marquette and 2nd Ave. and has recently added three new commuter trails to its system (some still in process). For information on commuter routes, locker locations, etc. for both Minneapolis and St. Paul, call Metro Commuter Services at 651-602-1602.

Following are some agencies that may be helpful in providing more information on urban trails.

### Minneapolis Department of Public Works Transportation Trails
In addition to trails administered by the Parks Department, Minneapolis Public Works initiates and administers several urban trails. Probably the most notable among them to date is the Cedar Lake Trail into downtown Minneapolis (see page 129).

### Hennepin County Parks

Several Hennepin County Parks have paved bike trails. These trails are open to the public from 5 AM until sunset. There is also an enforced speed limit of 15 miles per hour. For trail information, contact Hennepin County Parks, 12615 County Road 9, Plymouth, MN 55441-1248, 612-559-9000.

### Ramsey County Parks

Ramsey County Parks are open one-half hour before sunrise and close one-half hour after sunset While the county parks generally do not offer paved trails, the regional parks do. For trail information, contact Ramsey County Parks and Recreation, 2015 N. Van Dyke St., Maplewood, MN 55109, 651-745-2500.

### CITIES WITH ADDITIONAL BIKING OPPORTUNITIES

The following cities have at least some biking opportunities. For more information about biking opportunities in these communities, be sure to contact their Chamber of Commerces and Tourist offices.

### Apple Valley 612-953-2300

You can tour much of Apple Valley on paved off-road trails. This would include the Minnesota Zoo and into Lebanon Hills Regional Park. (see page 158)

### Bloomington 612-948-8877

The city of Bloomington provides many miles of off-road paved bicycle paths, especially in the Bush Lake, Hyland Lake and Normandale Lake areas.

### Brooklyn Center 612-569-3382

This is the site of several very scenic off-road trails in the Palmer Lake area, paralleling Shingle Creek. Ride all the way from Brooklyn Park city limits to Minneapolis city limits safe from vehicle traffic.

### Brooklyn Park 612-493-8350

Brooklyn Park has some excellent asphalt trails, especially in Brookdale, Palmer Lake Park, and along the Edinbrook drainage channel. The city also includes most of the North Hennepin Trail Corridor. (See page 176)

### Burnsville 612-895-4504

Limited off-road trails but several miles of marked street shoulder.

### Champlin 612-421-2820/8100

The city of Champlin has limited off-road bicycle trails but has plans for expansion.

**Chaska** 612-448-5633 ext. 105
This city has made major strides in providing both off-road and street-side bicycle paths. It also has access to, or is close to three regional rail-trails, the North and South Corridors of the LRT to Hopkins and back to Victoria and the Minnesota Valley State Trail to Shakopee.

**Eagan** 651-681-4660
Another community with extensive off-road trails, offering 17.6 miles of 8' paved north-south trails and 15½ miles of east-west trails.

**Eden Prairie** 612-949-8441
Eden Prairie has one of the most extensive bicycle trail systems in the area.

**Fridley** 612-572-3570
Fridley combines road shoulder trails with several miles of off-road stretches.

**Hastings** 651-437-4127
Although Hastings off-road trails are not extensive, you will find some very attractive ones. They are augmented by several miles of marked road shoulder.

**Inver Grove Heights** 651-450-2587
Excellent off-road trails throughout the urban area.

**Lakeville** 612-985-4600
The city paved trails are excellent and easy.

**Maple Grove** 612-494-6500
Maple Grove is continuing to expand its trail system.

**Mendota Heights** 651-452-1850
The city provides an extensive network of off-road paved trails. It also includes the 4.2 mile Big Rivers Regional Trail in Mendota (see page 135). Via the Mendota Bridge, this will also provide another link with the Minneapolis Trails.

**Minnetonka** 612-939-8203
Minnetonka is part of the Minnetonka Loop Trail System and connections are available to both the north corridor of the LRT and the Luce Line State Trail, on the north.

**Plymouth** 612-509-5200
Although a lot of Plymouth's bicycle paths are road shoulder and sidewalk, several miles of off-road are dispersed throughout the area.

**Robbinsdale** 612-531-1278
To date, Robbinsdale has relatively limited off-road bikeways.

**Rosemount** 612-888-0957
Rosemount trails are concentrated in the western edge of the city with paved trails being somewhat limited.

**Roseville** 651-415-2100
Roseville has expanded its off-road trail system. A north-south ride paralleling Lexington Avenue and east-west along County Road C are especially fine urban rides.

**Shoreview** 651-490-4600
Shoreview has over 15 miles of paved, mostly roadside, but well-marked trails. Snail Lake Park provides some excellent off-road rides.

**Woodbury** 651-714-3583
Woodbury has done a great job of trail construction within its urban area. You will find their trails paved and well-marked with most parallel, but separate, from roads and streets.

**WHERE:** Hastings
**LENGTH:** 4 miles
**SURFACE:** Paved
**TRAIL USE:**

**Access:** From St. Paul, go 9 miles east on I-94 then 7 miles south on County Road 15, 3 miles east on County Road 20.

Four miles of paving in a scenic setting along the St. Croix River and near Afton Alps ski area make this park well worth bringing your bicycle. Other park trails are quite rugged, offering a challenging hike or cross-country ski. The park offers hiking, swimming, fishing, boating, volleyball court, horseshoe pit, picnicing, golfing, winter skiing (downhill at nearby Afton Alps) and snowmobiling.

The native prairie is being restored in several areas in the park. A fun hike can start at the Interpretive Center, follow a self-guided interpretive trail, climb the bluff, stop at scenic overlooks eventually circling back to swimming beach and picnic area. The leaves are spectacular in the fall and the river is a great place to watch hawks and eagles.

### Bike Shorts

Be alert to changing conditions. Rain will muffle the sound of approaching vehicles and generate slippery conditions, especially after a long period without rain. (Roadway oil and grime can be hazardous until the rain washes them away).

### FOR MORE INFORMATION:

Afton State Park
6959 Peller Avenue South
Hastings, MN 55033
651-436-5391

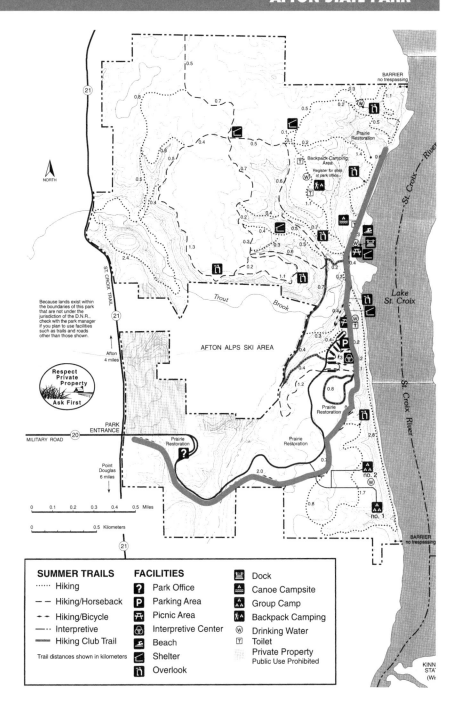

BARRIER
no trespassing

Prairie
Restoration

Backpack Camping
Area
Register for sites
at park office.

Lake
St. Croix

St. Croix River

St. Croix River

Trout Brook

AFTON ALPS SKI AREA

Because lands exist within
the boundaries of this park
that are not under the
jurisdiction of the D.N.R.,
check with the park manager
if you plan to use facilities
such as trails and roads
other than those shown.

ST CROIX TRAIL

Afton
4 miles

Respect
Private
Property
Ask First

PARK
ENTRANCE

MILITARY ROAD

Prairie
Restoration

Prairie
Restoration

Prairie
Restoration

Point
Douglas
6 miles

no. 2

no. 1

NORTH

| 0 | 0.1 | 0.2 | 0.3 | 0.4 | 0.5 Miles |

| 0 | | 0.5 Kilometers |

BARRIER
no trespassing

KINN
STAT
(Wis

## SUMMER TRAILS
- ...... Hiking
- – – Hiking/Horseback
- – – Hiking/Bicycle
- –·– Interpretive
- ▬▬ Hiking Club Trail

Trail distances shown in kilometers

## FACILITIES
- ❓ Park Office
- 🅿 Parking Area
- 🛱 Picnic Area
- ◎ Interpretive Center
- 🏖 Beach
- 🏠 Shelter
- 🔭 Overlook

- 🛏 Dock
- ⛺ Canoe Campsite
- 🏕 Group Camp
- 🏕 Backpack Camping
- Ⓦ Drinking Water
- Ⓣ Toilet
- ░ Private Property
  Public Use Prohibited

**WHERE:** Approx. 20 miles west of downtown Minneapolis on County Road 19, between Highway 12 and Highway 55

**LENGTH:** 6.2 miles

**SURFACE:** Paved

**TRAIL USE:** 🚲 🚶 🚻 ✈ ⛷ 🐎

**Access:** From Highway 12, take County Road 19 north and follow 19 to the main park entrance. From Highway 55, take County Road 24 west to County Road 19, turn south and follow 19 to the main park entrance, or take Highway 55 to county Road 19, turn south and follow 19 to the main entrance.

Terrain is somewhat rolling and the trail goes through woods as well as meadows. The park includes three lakes offering swimming, boating, fishing and golf in addition to its paved trails.

## Bike Shorts

When planning a trip, be aware of your own capabilities as well as the limitations and health of your friends. A ride which tests one's outer limits is best left to those conditioned to do so.

### FOR MORE INFORMATION:

Baker Park Reserve
Phone: 479-2258 (Gate)
476-466 (Office)

Hennepin Parks
12615 County Road 9
Plymouth, MN 55441
612-559-9000

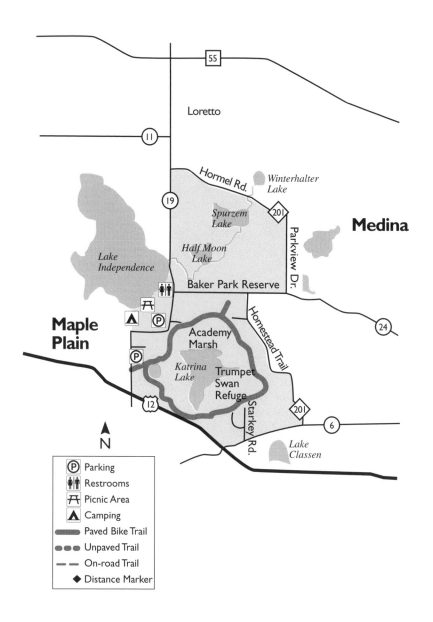

Loretto

Winterhalter Lake

*Spurzem Lake*

**Medina**

Hormel Rd.

*Half Moon Lake*

*Lake Independence*

Baker Park Reserve

**Maple Plain**

Parkview Dr.

Academy Marsh

Homestead Trail

*Katrina Lake*

Trumpet Swan Refuge

Starkey Rd.

*Lake Classen*

N

P Parking
Restrooms
Picnic Area
Camping
Paved Bike Trail
Unpaved Trail
On-road Trail
◆ Distance Marker

**WHERE:** Minneapolis
**LENGTH:** .3 miles
**SURFACE:** Paved, bicycle lanes minimum 14 ft. wide with parallel pedestrian lane minimum of 6 ft. wide.

**TRAIL USE:** 🚲 🚶 🛼

**Trailhead North:** Wirth Parkway, north of Highway 55.

**Trailhead South:** Connects with Cedar Lake Trail just west of the point where Cedar Lake Trail goes under I-394. Best parking is near Target Center, the Ice Arena, or the Sculpture Garden at the Walker Art Center.

Another new commuter trail administered by the Hennepin County Park Board provides a route from the northwest into the loop area. Plans include eventually extending it west to connect with the Luce Line DNR rail-trail. (See page 132.)

---

### Bike Shorts

Good water bottles are inexpensive and readily available. Be sure you carry ample water for your trip and use it often. Dehydration can sap your strength and may even cause more serious problems.

---

### FOR MORE INFORMATION:

Department of Public Works
Minneapolis City Hall, Room 233
Transportation Division
350 S. 5th St.
Minneapolis, MN 55415
612-673-2352

**WHERE:** Minneapolis
**LENGTH:** 5 miles
**SURFACE:** Paved, 10' wide, with separate paved walking trail

**TRAIL USE:** 🚲 🚶 🛼

**Trailhead West:** At Highway 100 and Cedar Lake Road, southbound on Highway 100, take Stephen Drive, exit right, and drive south to Minnetonka Boulevard, then back on frontage road to trail access, where there is minimal parking. If you are headed northbound on Highway 100, take the Cedar Lake Road exit.

**Mid Access:** At numerous locations, see map.

**Trailhead East:** In downtown Minneapolis, at 12th and Glenwood, just west of the Target Center. There is parking available at the 7th Street Garage.

This is the first route in the state constructed especially for non-motorized commuting. This trail is administered by the Minneapolis Department of Public Works, Transportation and Special Projects Division.

Utilizing federal transportation funds, this trail has a higher speed limit and includes a separate paved trail for skaters, runners and walkers to facilitate its basic purpose of commuting. It is now the most heavily-used trail in the entire Metro Area.

The separation of bicycles from foot traffic is not unique, but it is the first case where the entire trail is so designed. Efforts toward building dual trails in congested areas is becoming a reality, and would certainly be a safety improvement. (See page 132.)

---

### *FOR MORE INFORMATION:*

Department of Public Works
Minneapolis City Hall, Room 233
Transportation Division
350 S. 5th St.
Minneapolis, MN 55415
612-673-2352

**WHERE:** Minneapolis
**LENGTH:** 1.5 miles
**SURFACE:** Paved, bicycle lanes minimum 14 ft. wide with paralleled pedestrian minimum of 6 ft. wide

**TRAIL USE:**

**South Trailhead:** There is a small parking lot southeast of 28th Street but this trail terminates where it joins the Midtown Greenway Trail. There is no direct access at this point.

**North Trailhead:** This trail connects the Cedar Lake Trail and the Midtown Greenway Trail with no direct access where it joins the Cedar Lake Trail (see east access for Cedar Lake Trail as closest access point).

Another commuter trail located on a route leased from the Regional Railroad Authority. It provides a direct link between the Cedar Lake commuter trail and Midtown Greenway. (See page 132.)

---

## Bike Shorts

The old Irish prayer "May the wind blow always at your back" is only partially true for bicyclists. Be prepared for the vacuum effect of passing vehicles, sudden gusts or sudden absences when passing roadside buildings, trees or other shelter.

---

### FOR MORE INFORMATION:

Department of Public Works
Minneapolis City Hall, Room 233
Transportation Division
350 S. 5th St.
Minneapolis, MN 55415
612-673-2352

**WHERE:** Minneapolis
**LENGTH:** 5.6 miles (when completed)
**SURFACE:** Paved–bicycle lanes minimum 14 ft. wide with parallel pedestrian lane minimum of 6 ft. wide

**TRAIL USE:** 🚲 🚶 🛼

**West Trailhead:** Trail joins the Kenilworth Trail near 31st and Chowen Avenue (no designated parking).

**Mid Access:** Dean Avenue west of Lake of the Isles. Southeast corner of Lake of the Isles where it connects to the Lake trail system. At James, Irving and Humboldt there are grade level entrances but the trail drops below grade for the next several blocks with access only at Bryant Avenue South and Nicollet Avenue Street parking.

**East Trailhead:** Currently at Nicollet Avenue When Phase II is implemented, additional access will be included. Street parking.

A new multi-use trail paralleling the 29th Street rail corridor in south Minneapolis. As yet, there are limited public facilities and parking except at Lake of the Isles. The right of the way is leased from the Regional Authority and will be administered by the City of Minneapolis. It will provide a non-stop corridor from Chowen Avenue to Nicollet, continuing east to Hiawatha Avenue when Phase II is completed. Phase III, extending all the way to the Mississippi River is planned for the future. (See page 132.)

---

### *FOR MORE INFORMATION:*

Department of Public Works
Minneapolis City Hall, Room 233
Transportation Division
350 S. 5th St.
Minneapolis, MN 55415
612-673-2352

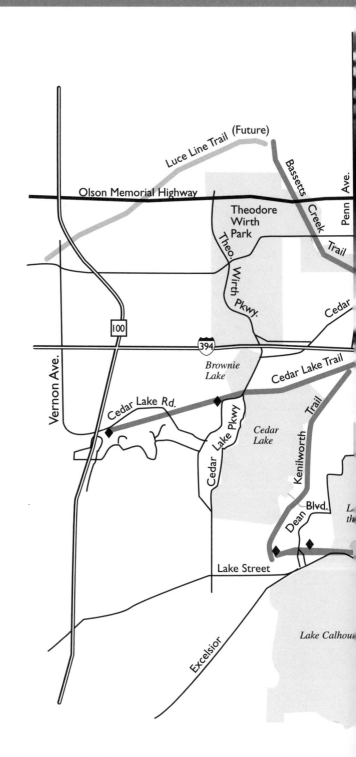

Broadway

Washington Ave.

North
Minneapolis

55

nwood Ave.

Road

Bassetts Creek

Linden Ave.

Hennepin Ave.

Target
Center Ⓟ

Downtown
Minneapolis

Ⓟ Parade
Ice
Garden

Ⓟ

Logan

Douglas Ave.

94

Hennepin Ave.

Bryant Ave. S.

Nicollet Ave.

35W

5th Ave. S.

◆◆◆ Midtown ◆ Greenway
Lagoon Ave.   29th St.

◆ *(Phase II-to Hiawatha)*

| Ⓟ Parking | ▬▬▬ Paved Bike Trail |
|---|---|
| 🚻 Restrooms | ●●● Unpaved Trail |
| ⛱ Picnic Area | – – On-road Trail |
| ⛺ Camping | ◆ Trail Access |

N

133 Metro

**WHERE:** Maplewood
**LENGTH:** 1.75 miles
**SURFACE:** Paved, 12' wide
**TRAIL USE:** 🚴 🚶 ♿ ⛷️

**Trailhead West:** At the Point Douglas Road Bikeway/Battle Creek Park Entrance Road. You will find a large parking lot here.

**Trailhead East:** At Battle Creek Park, east of the McKnight Road Bike Path. There is a parking lot here.

### FOR MORE INFORMATION:

Ramsey County Parks & Recreation
2015 Van Dyke St.
Maplewood, Minnesota 55109
651-748-2500

**WHERE:** Lilydale, Mendota and Mendota Heights
**LENGTH:** 4.2 miles
**SURFACE:** Asphalt, 10' wide
**TRAIL USE:** 🚴 🚶 🛼

**Trailhead North:** The trail begins at Lilydale Park, just where it crosses under I-35E. Parking and facilities are available here.

**Trailhead South:** At Pilot Knob Road and Trunk Highway 13 in Mendota Heights. Limited parking here.

The Big River Trail was constructed by Dakota County and opened in the late fall of 1995. It is also administered by Dakota County and has rapidly become a very popular addition to the urban trail system. It follows the old Soo line rail bed and is surprisingly scenic.

Of special interest is an overlook just off Old Trunk Highway 13 which is difficult to get to except by this trail. Parking is available where Mendota Heights Road ends on the Sibley Memorial Highway. There is a paved connection from this lot to the main trail. Parking is also provided in Mendota near the historical marker just below St. Peter Church.

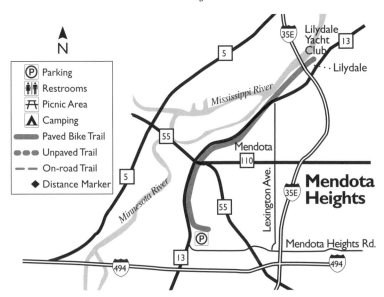

### FOR MORE INFORMATION:

Mendota Heights City Hall
1101 Victoria Curve
Mendota Heights, MN 55118
651-452-1850

# BUNKER HILL REGIONAL PARK

**WHERE:** Anoka County-Coon Rapids
**LENGTH:** 5.5 miles
**SURFACE:** Paved
**TRAIL USE:**

**Access:** Park entrance off County Roads A, B and D.

The park includes a variety of activities including archery and the Bunker Hills Stables complete with guided horse trail riding and hay and sleigh rides. The Bunker Hills Golf Course is here as well as picnic pavilions and sites for camping. A very popular summer feature is the Wave Pool with its air-generated waves, the first of its kind in the state. Bunker Hills was one of the first parks in the regional system.

## Bike Shorts

Obey traffic laws and obey traffic signs. Most serious accidents involve motor vehicles. Drivers are conditioned to expect you to do as another motor vehicle would.

## *FOR MORE INFORMATION:*

Anoka County Parks
550 N.W. Bunker Lake Blvd.
Anoka, MN 55304
612-757-3920

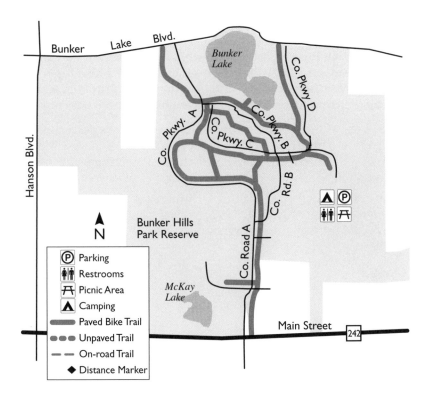

**WHERE:** St. Paul
**LENGTH:** 6 miles
**SURFACE:** 12 feet paved
**TRAIL USE:**

This is a new trail with the southern 6 miles at or near completion. The northern section (to downtown White Bear Lake) is funded and right-of-way negotiations are in progress.

The Burlington Northern Trail connects to the Phalen Creek Trail just south of Lake Phalen at the intersection of Wheelock Parkway, Johnson Parkway and East Shore Drive. The latter is also built on the Burlington Northern rail bed and combining both trails into one ride permits a 10½ mile off-road ride through residential St. Paul.

There are plans to surface the 1½ miles from Johnson Parkway north to Frost Avenue. The 2½ miles from Frost Avenue to Beam Avenue is already complete, with the north end presently terminating near Maplewood Mall.

This is an excellent off-road trail in an urban setting. It provides a connection to the Gateway DNR Trail and will eventually become an off-road trail all the way from downtown St. Paul to downtown White Bear Lake.

---

### FOR MORE INFORMATION:

Ramsey County Parks and Recreation Department
2015 North VanDyke Street
Maplewood, MN 55109
651-748-2500

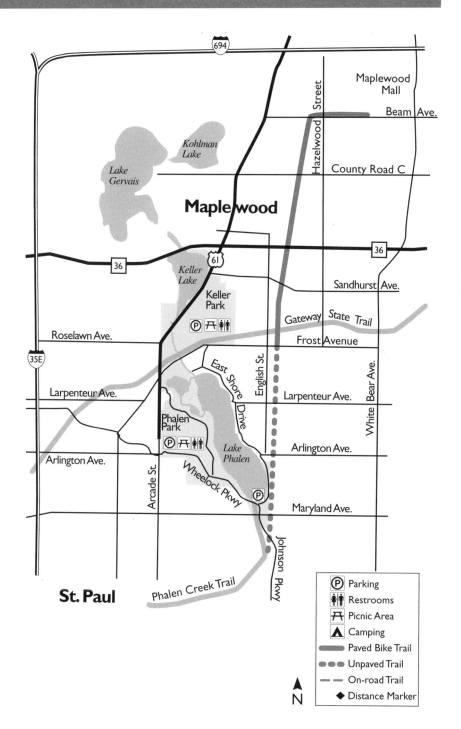

**WHERE:** Victoria
**LENGTH:** 7.65 miles
**SURFACE:** Paved
**TRAIL USE:** 🚲 🚶 🏕 ➡ 🎿 🐎

**Access:** Located in Victoria, on Carver County Road 11. Take Highway 7 west from Minneapolis and turn left on County Road 11. Or take Highway 5 west from Minneapolis and turn right on County Road 11.

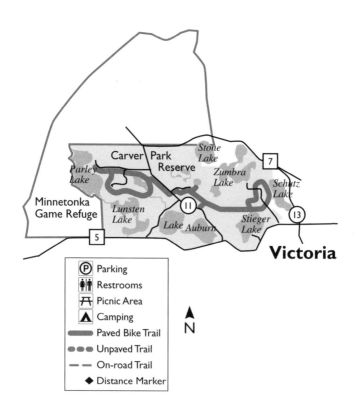

**FOR MORE INFORMATION:**

Hennepin Parks
12615 County Road 9
Plymouth, MN 55441
612-559-9000

Nature Center
612-472-4911
Gate
612-446-9474

**WHERE:** Prior Lake
**LENGTH:** 3.5 miles
**SURFACE:** Paved
**TRAIL USE:** 🚴 🥾 🏕️ 🛶 ⛷️

**Access:** Located near Prior Lake on Scott County Road 27. From I-35W, go west on County Road 42, then south on County Road 27. Or take I-494 to County Road 18, go south on 18 to Highway. 101, then east to Highway 13, south on 13 to County Road 42, east on 42 to County Road 27, and south on 27 to the park entrance.

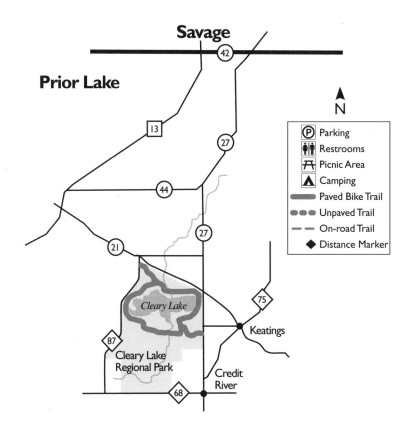

**Savage**

**Prior Lake**

N

| | |
|---|---|
| Ⓟ | Parking |
| 🚻 | Restrooms |
| 🏞️ | Picnic Area |
| ⛺ | Camping |
| ▬ | Paved Bike Trail |
| ●●● | Unpaved Trail |
| – – | On-road Trail |
| ◆ | Distance Marker |

*Cleary Lake*

Keatings

Cleary Lake
Regional Park

Credit
River

---

### FOR MORE INFORMATION:

Hennepin Parks
12615 County Road 9
Plymouth, MN 55441
612-559-9000

Visitor Center
612-447-2171

**WHERE:** Medicine Lake
**LENGTH:** 2 miles
**SURFACE:** Paved
**TRAIL USE:** 🚴 🚶 ⛺ 🎿

**Access:** Take exit 22 east off I-494 (at County Road 9) in Plymouth to park entrance.

Although limited trail distance now, plans include expanding a connection east to Theodore Wirth Park where links will eventually connect to the several metro area trails.

### *FOR MORE INFORMATION:*

Hennepin Parks
12615 County Road 9
Plymouth, MN 55441
612-559-9000

Clifton E. French Park
612-559-9000

**WHERE:** St. Paul
**LENGTH:** 1.8 miles
**SURFACE:** Paved
**TRAIL USE:** 🚴 🚶 ⛉

**Access:** Off Como Avenue or Lexington Parkway.

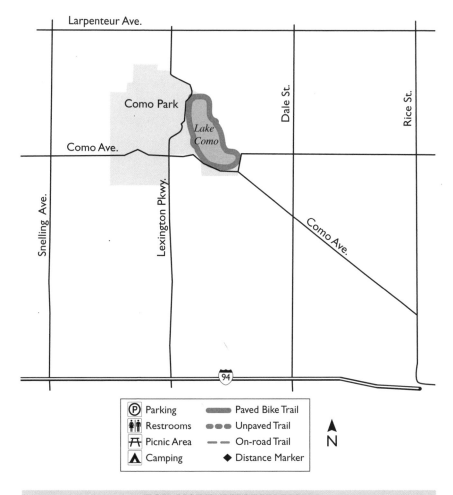

**FOR MORE INFORMATION:**

St. Paul Parks & Recreation
300 City Hall Annex
St. Paul, MN 55102
651-266-6400

**WHERE:** Coon Rapids
**LENGTH:** 3 miles
**SURFACE:** Asphalt, 8' wide
**TRAIL USE:** 🚴 🚶 ⛺

**Access:** Use the main entrance off Egret Boulevard.

Ample parking and facilities are available in this Anoka County Park.

This is a multi-use park, with one of its main features being the Coon Rapids Dam which terminates near the Visitor Center. A biking/walking path across the bridge will connect with the North Hennepin Regional Trail in Brooklyn Park. At the southern end of the trail, you will connect directly to the 8 miles of the Mississippi Regional Trail Corridor traversing Fridley and Columbia Heights.

*FOR MORE INFORMATION:*

Anoka County Parks
550 N.W. Bunker Lake Blvd.
Anoka, MN 55304
612-757-3920

**WHERE:** St. Paul
**LENGTH:** 6.7 miles
**SURFACE:** Paved, 10' wide
**TRAIL USE:** 🚲 🚶 📷

**Trailhead North:** At Mississippi River Boulevard and Hidden Falls Drive. There are large parking lots along Hidden Falls Drive and along Crosby Farm Road.

**Trailhead East:** At Shepherd Road and Crosby Lake Road. There is a small parking lot here.

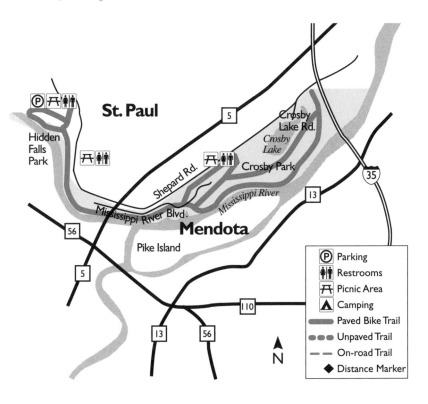

## FOR MORE INFORMATION:

St. Paul Parks & Recreation
300 City Hall Annex
St. Paul, MN 55102
651-266-6400

**WHERE:** Osseo
**LENGTH:** 9.3 miles, paved (Also a 6.5 mile paved North Hennepin Trail corridor connects the Elm Creek trails with the Coon Rapids Dam.)
**SURFACE:** Paved
**TRAIL USE:**

**Access:** Located northwest of Osseo, between the communities of Champlin, Dayton and Maple Grove. For the recreation area, take County Road 81 to Territorial Road. Turn right and follow to the park entrance.

A 5-mile turf trail is open for mountain biking; the designated mountain bike trail is the only turf trail in the reserve where bikes are permitted.

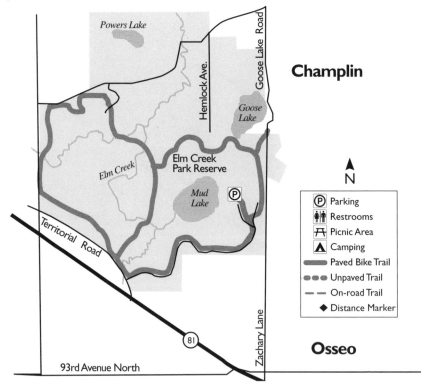

## FOR MORE INFORMATION:

Hennepin Parks
12615 County Road 9
Plymouth, MN 55441
612-559-9000

Visitor Center
612-424-5511

**WHERE:** Maple Grove
**LENGTH:** 1.9 mile
**SURFACE:** Paved
**TRAIL USE:** 🚴 🚶 🛼 ⛷

**Access:** Exit Highway I-494 west at Bass Lake Road in Maple Grove.

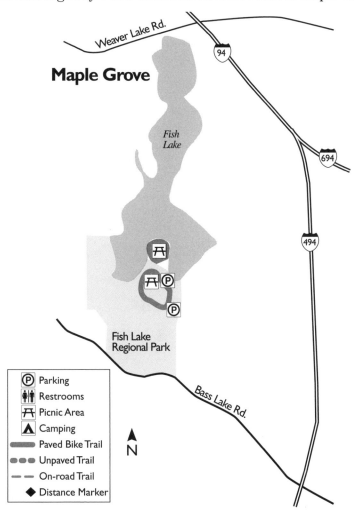

Weaver Lake Rd.

94

**Maple Grove**

*Fish Lake*

694

494

Fish Lake
Regional Park

Bass Lake Rd.

| | |
|---|---|
| Ⓟ | Parking |
| 🚹🚺 | Restrooms |
| 🛇 | Picnic Area |
| ⛺ | Camping |
| ▬▬ | Paved Bike Trail |
| ●●● | Unpaved Trail |
| – – | On-road Trail |
| ◆ | Distance Marker |

▲
N

## FOR MORE INFORMATION:

Hennepin Parks
12615 County Road 9
Plymouth, MN 55441
612-559-9000

Visitor Center
612-420-3423

**WHERE:** Highway 5 and Post Road near Minneapolis/ St.Paul Airport
**LENGTH:** 5 miles
**SURFACE:** Paved
**TRAIL USE:**

**Trailhead North:** Connects to the Minneapolis trail system via the Minnehaha trail access from the parking lot at the Bishop Whipple Building on the north side of Highway 55 across from Fort Snelling itself. Facilities during open hours.

**Trailhead South:** At the Park entrance. Take the Post Road exit east off Highway 5. A State Park is fee required to park. You will find full park facilities here.

A short but scenic ride which can be combined with the Minnehaha Trail for a longer river valley ride. Eventually, the Minnesota Valley State Park Trail is planned to connect with this one.

## Bike Shorts

Watch for road debris or loose rocks or gravel. Slow down if there is excessive debris or broken road surface. Learn to guide your bike very straight and vertical through loose sand or rocks. If you find a short stretch of loose sand it would even pay to practice riding through it a few times to give you needed confidence when it surprises you along the way.

### FOR MORE INFORMATION:

Fort Snelling State Park
Highway 5 and Post Road
St. Paul, MN 55111
651-725-2390

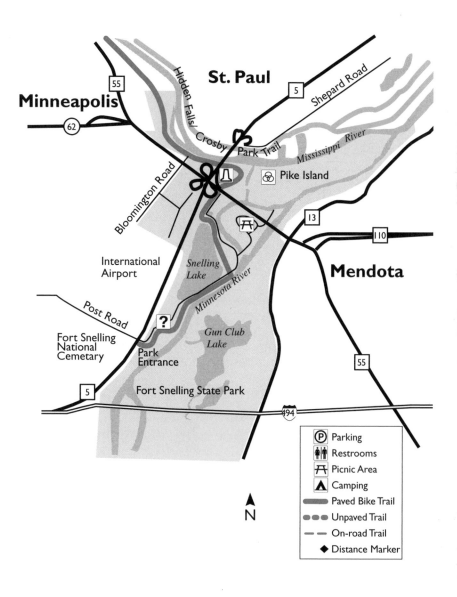

Minneapolis

St. Paul

55

62

Hidden Falls/

Crosby Park Trail

5

Shepard Road

Mississippi River

Pike Island

Bloomington Road

13

110

International
Airport

Snelling
Lake

Minnesota River

Mendota

Post Road

?

Fort Snelling
National
Cemetary

Park
Entrance

Gun Club
Lake

55

5

Fort Snelling State Park

494

N

| | |
|---|---|
| Ⓟ | Parking |
| 🚻 | Restrooms |
| ⛺ | Picnic Area |
| ⛺ | Camping |
| | Paved Bike Trail |
| ●●● | Unpaved Trail |
| — — | On-road Trail |
| ◆ | Distance Marker |

**WHERE:** St. Paul to Pine Point Park
**LENGTH:** 18 miles
**SURFACE:** Paved
**TRAIL USE:** 🚴 🚶 🛶 ⛷ 🐎

**Trailhead West:** Take the Maryland exit off I-35E just north of downtown St. Paul. Go east one block to Westminster Avenue, turn north to Arlington Avenue. It is about one-half block west on Arlington to a paved parking lot on the south side of the street. Vandalism has not permitted portable toilets.

Note: The trail actually dead ends 1.1 mile west on Cayuga Avenue after crossing over I-35E, but with street parking only in residential area.

**Mid Access:** The trail is accessible from a number of streets and city parks. Phalen-Keller Regional Park has parking available and you can add 2.9 miles of paved trail. See map, page 178. In Maplewood, Flicek Park on Frost Avenue has parking available. Near the junction of Highway 36 and I-694 in Oakdale, there is a paved parking lot and portable restrooms. From Highway 36 go south one-quarter block on Hadley Avenue to 55th Street North. Go east on 55th Street one-half mile to parking area on right. In Pine Springs, from Highway 36 go north on Hilton Avenue, and take first right onto High Trail Avenue North. Parking is available in the cul-de-sac. There is a parking lot on the south side of Highway 96 just west of the intersection of Highway 96 and Kimbro Avenue North.

**Trailhead East:** Although the trail continues a short distance east (not paved), the best access and parking is at Pine Point Park. Approximately five miles north of Stillwater on Highway 55 (Norell Avenue North) on the west side of the road. Washington County charges a fee for parking. There are portable restrooms here.

The Gateway Trail's wide surface, easy access and excellent parking facilities provide a first-class trail with more side trip options than most. The metropolitan location, especially the west 8.3 miles, make it one of the more popular multi-use trails. Expect more than the usual amount of foot, skater and wheelchair traffic on the western half. With the cooperation of MN DOT, an overpass over I-35E was recently completed especially for this trail. This made possible a 1.1 mile extension and opens the way to link with the St. Paul Grand Rounds Trail and Capitol Complex.

You will find this to be a ride of contrasts. The west half winds through concentrated residential sections, along or through city parks and golf courses and crosses some busy streets. The eastern half passes through more open country, light traffic roads and lighter trail use. You may encounter horseback riders as the DNR has included a riding path paralleling the bike trail on the section north of I-694.

At just under 17 miles, this is a good trail for a ride both ways in one day. There are many opportunities for side trips to lengthen your ride. Phalen-Keller Regional Park has 2.9 miles of paved trail. You can ride either west to Mahtomedi or east to Stillwater on the paved Washington County trail that intersects with the Gateway at Washington County #12. When you reach Pine Point Park you will see a Washington County paved trail along #55 (Norell Avenue) both north and south for several miles.

Excellent bridges with no more than a 5% grade take you up and over two of the busiest streets (McKnight and White Bear). Expect to cross numerous city streets and a few county roads. Also, note a darker than usual surface on sections of this trail. The DNR is experimenting with a surface of shredded junk tires and pulverized shingles as aggregate mix rather than gravel in the bituminous. Both the DOT and the DNR are still evaluating its possibilities.

## FOR MORE INFORMATION:

DNR Trail Office
1200 Warner Road
St. Paul, MN 55106
651-772-7935

St. Paul Chamber of Commerce
332 Minnesota St.
#N-205
St. Paul, MN 55101
651-223-5000

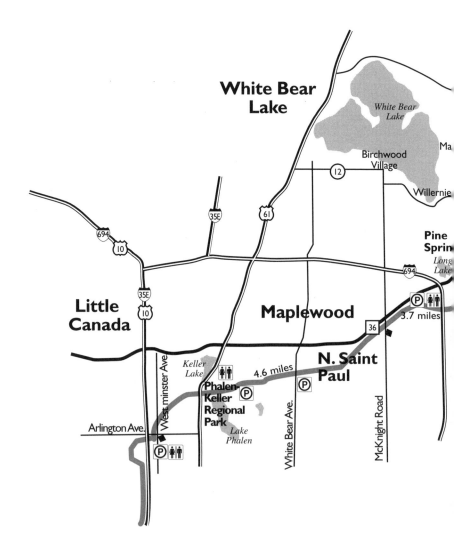

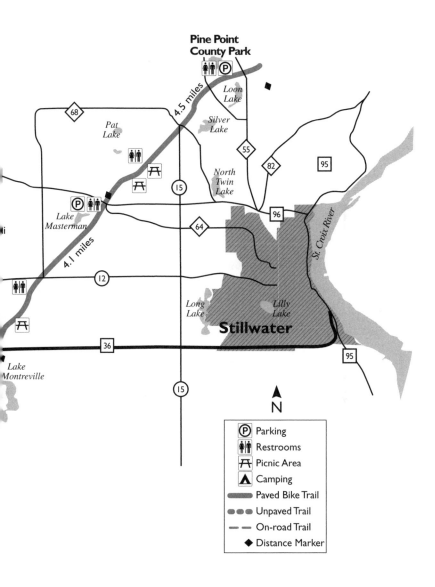

**Pine Point County Park**

Loon Lake

Silver Lake

Pat Lake

North Twin Lake

Lake Masterman

4.5 miles

4.1 miles

Long Lake

Lilly Lake

**Stillwater**

Lake Montreville

St. Croix River

68

55

82

95

15

64

96

12

36

15

95

N

| | |
|---|---|
| Ⓟ | Parking |
| 🚻 | Restrooms |
| ⊞ | Picnic Area |
| ▲ | Camping |
| ▬▬ | Paved Bike Trail |
| ●●● | Unpaved Trail |
| – – | On-road Trail |
| ◆ | Distance Marker |

Administered by Minnesota Department of Natural Resources

**WHERE:** City of Hastings
**LENGTH:** 3 miles
**SURFACE:** Paved
**TRAIL USE:** 🚴 🚶 ⛷️

**Access:** Various city streets (see map below).

Although Hasting's off-road trails are not extensive, you will find some very attractive ones. They are augmented by several miles of marked road shoulder.

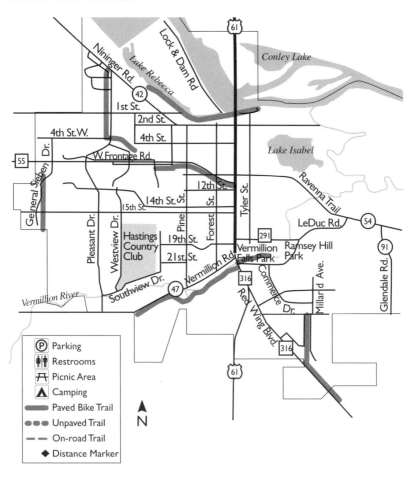

---

### FOR MORE INFORMATION:

| | |
|---|---|
| Hastings Chamber of Commerce<br>651-437-6775 | Hastings City Hall<br>651-437-4127 |

**WHERE:** Bloomington
**LENGTH:** 5.5 miles
**SURFACE:** Paved
**TRAIL USE:** 🚴 🚶 🎿 ⛷️

**Access:** Located on East Bush Lake Road in Bloomington. From I-494, go south on Normandale Boulevard (Highway 100) to 84th Street. Turn right and follow 84th Street to East Bush Lake Road. Go south on East Bush Lake Road and follow the signs to Richardson Nature Center and Hyland Visitor Center.

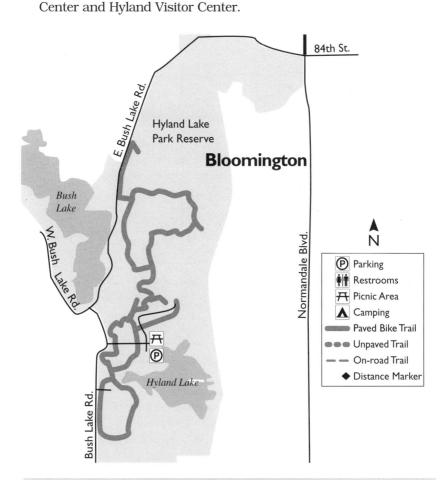

**FOR MORE INFORMATION:**

Hyland Park Office
612-941-4362

Hennepin Parks
12615 County Rd. 9
Plymouth, MN 55441
612-559-9000

**WHERE:** St. Paul
**LENGTH:** 3 miles
**SURFACE:** Paved, 8' wide
**TRAIL USE:**

**Trailhead North:** At Keller Park there are parking lots on both sides of Highway 61, just north of the Munger Gateway State Trail.

**Trailhead South:** At the intersection of Wheelock Parkway, Johnson Parkway, and East Shore Drive, at the south end of Lake Phalen, where there is a small parking lot. There are also four large parking lots along Phalen Drive, north of Wheelock Parkway, in Phalen Park.

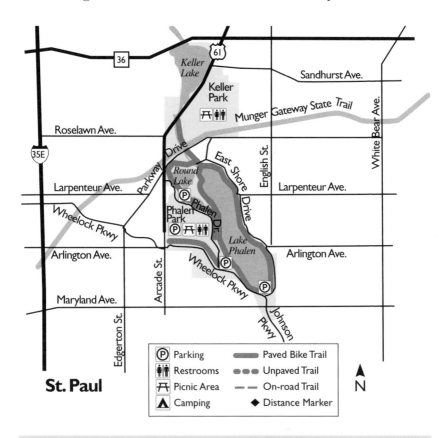

### FOR MORE INFORMATION:

Phalen Center
1000 E. Wheelock Parkway
St. Paul, MN 55106
651-298-5721

St. Paul Parks & Recreation
300 City Hall Annex
St. Paul, MN 55102
651-266-6400

**WHERE:** West Minneapolis
**LENGTH:** 6.5 miles
**SURFACE:** Paved
**TRAIL USE:** 🚴 🚶 🏕️ 🛶 ⛷️ 🐎

**Access:** Located approximately 30 miles west of Minneapolis on County Road 50. Take Highway 55 west to County Road 50, turn left and follow to the park entrance.

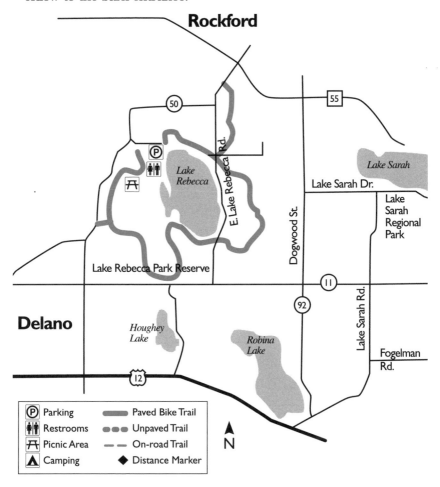

FOR MORE INFORMATION:

612-475-4666

Hennepin Parks
12615 County Rd. 9
Plymouth, MN 55441
612-559-9000

**WHERE:** Eagan, west section; Apple Valley, east section
**LENGTH:** 4.2 miles in west section, 6.5 miles in east section
**SURFACE:** Paved
**TRAIL USE:** 🚲 🚶 🏕️ 🛶 ⛷️ 🐎

**Access:** Parking and facilities are available off Johnny Cake Ridge Road, Pilot Knob Road and Cliff Road.

The two sections of this park are popular for hiking, horseback riding and camping, so expect some traffic on the trails. The west section of the park is adjacent to the Minnesota Zoo.

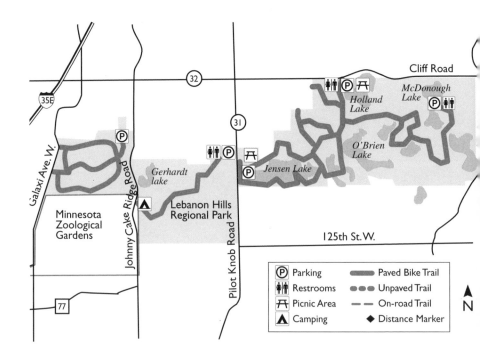

**WHERE:** New Brighton
**LENGTH:** Approximately 3 miles
**SURFACE:** Paved 8' wide
**TRAIL USE:** 🚴 🚶 🏕️

**Trailhead West:** At the park entrance off Long Lake Road. Take the Long Lake Road exit off I-694. You will find parking and facilities here.

**Trailhead East:** At Highway 96 and old Highway 8. There is limited parking here, in addition to an interesting off-road trail which can be extended northwest to Long Lake Road.

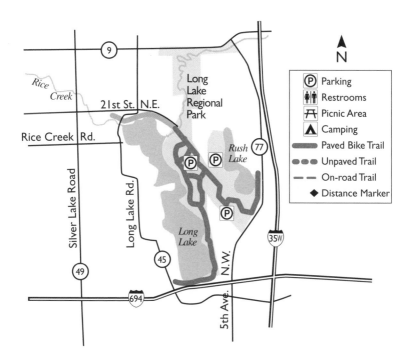

### FOR MORE INFORMATION:

New Brighton Parks
400-10th Street N.W.
New Brighton, MN 55112
651-638-2120

**WHERE:** St. Paul-Maplewood

**LENGTH:** 5 miles

**SURFACE:** On-street bike lanes from the Point Douglas Road Bikeway (near Highway 61) on the west to I-494 and from I-494 to Tower Road in Woodbury.

**TRAIL USE:** 🚴 🚶 ♿ 🛼 ⛷ 🏇

**Trailhead West:** At Lower Afton and the Point Douglas Road Bikeway section of the Mississippi River Trail. There is a parking lot at the north end of Point Douglas Road at Battle Creek.

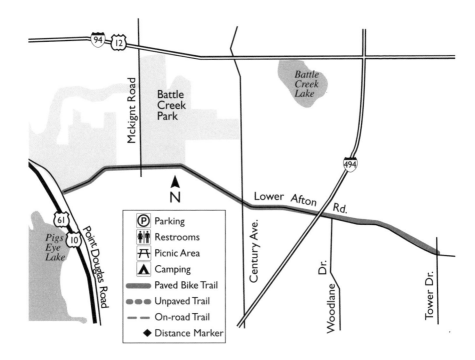

---

### *FOR MORE INFORMATION:*

Maplewood City Hall
1830 E. Co. Road B
Maplewood, MN 55109
651-770-4500

## Accessories

Realizing there are a multitude of accessories available, we will confine our comments to a very few which we have found to be most beneficial to our biking safety and pleasure. Of course, the most important is a good helmet but we also suggest the following to increase your comfort and enjoyment.

1) Seat pads filled with gel provide multiple return on the investment in the form of added comfort.

2) Padded bike shorts reduce chafing, absorb moisture and provide additional padding.

3) A rear view mirror (either helmet or handle bar mounted) is primarily a safety accessory but it also saves neck strain.

4) Padded gloves help reduce discomfort of weight and tension on the hands when subject to long periods in the same position.

5) Frame-mounted water bottle should be translucent to keep track of supply.

**WHERE:** St. Paul
**LENGTH:** 4 miles
**SURFACE:** Paved 10' wide
**TRAIL USE:** 🚴 🚶 📷

**Trailhead South:** At McKnight and Lower Afton Road. There are parking lots in Battle Creek Park. This trail connects to the Battle Creek Regional Trail (see page 134) and Lower Afton Trail (see page 160).

**Trailhead North:** At McKnight and Larpenteur.

The McKnight Road Bike Path has few problems with cross traffic because it follows the west edge of Battle creek Park, the west edge of the 3M complex, the east edge of Beaver Lake Park, and the east edge of Hillcrest Golf Course (the 14th tee at Hillcrest, at 1070 feet above sea level, is the highest point in St. Paul). Following the Mississippi River Trail south from the Minnesota Fish Hatchery to the Battle Creek Trail, and then east to the McKnight Road Bike Path, continue north to Larpenteur. Follow the striped/signed on-street bike lanes on Larpenteur west to Lake Phalen. The Lake Phalen Park Trail south to Wheelock Parkway can provide a longer alternative to the Johnson Parkway section of the St. Paul Grand Rounds Bikeway System.

---

### *FOR MORE INFORMATION:*

St. Paul Parks & Recreation
300 City Hall Annex
St. Paul, MN 55102
651-266-6400

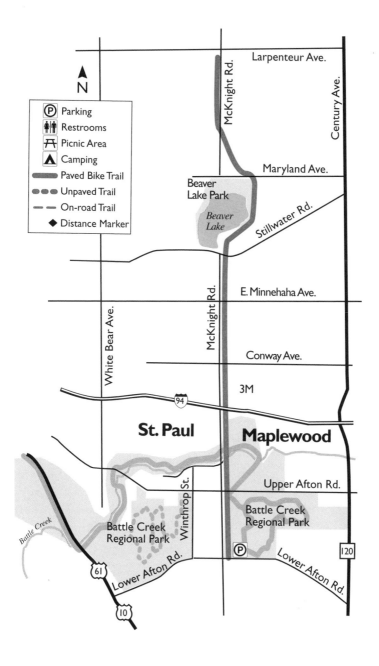

**WHERE:** Minneapolis
**LENGTH:** 37.9 miles
**SURFACE:** Asphalt
**TRAIL USE:**

## Biking The Grand Rounds
Submitted by Mary Lynn Pulscher, Minneapolis Parks Planning

The Grand Rounds of the Minneapolis parkway system offers a multitude of diverse amenities and beautiful scenery, including the Mississippi River, the Chain of Lakes and Minnehaha Falls. The Grand Rounds can provide you with a unique tour of one of America's finest urban park systems.

This is a recreational bike path system - the speed limit is 10 mph. Bike paths around Lakes Harriet, Calhoun and Isles are one direction. All other paths in the Grand Rounds are two-directional. Please stay to the right when riding and pass only on the left. You are allowed to bike on the parkways where the speed limit is 25 mph. The bike paths run in close proximity to the parkways, so where gaps exist in the path system it is possible to make connections using the road.

Bikes and in-line skate rentals are available along Lake Street in the Uptown area on the east side of Lake Calhoun.

Bike paths are accessible from any section of the Grand Rounds. There is a small daily fee to use the parking lots at Minnehaha Park, Boom Island and Lakes Nokomis, Harriet, Calhoun and Cedar. Free parking is available in these locations along the parkways in 'bays' and on nearby city streets. Locations not listed here have free parking in general.

During the summer, concessions are available at Minnehaha Park, Lake Nokomis, Lake Harriet, Lake Calhoun and at the Wirth Chalet. Drinking fountains and restrooms are also available at these sites. Because this trail system is located in an urban area you are never really far away from restaurants, restrooms or phones.

### The Chain of Lakes - Harriet, Calhoun, Isles and Cedar

### Lake Harriet Segment
Length: 2.9 miles
The amenities here include beaches, fishing and sailing docks, playgrounds, tennis courts, picnic areas and concessions. While riding along the east shore, take time to visit the second oldest rose garden in the U.S. with its two historic water display fountains as well as adjacent perennial garden, rock garden and Roberts Bird Sanctuary. If you're out riding on a summer evening stop by the Lake Harriet street-

car or take a boat ride on the Queen of the Lakes. Come back in the winter for ice-fishing, ice skating and cross country skiing.

## Lake Calhoun Segment
Length: 3.1 miles
Tired of biking? Rent a canoe at the refectory on the east side and explore Calhoun, Isles, Cedar and Brownie Lakes. Or take in a volleyball game at Thomas Beach on the southwest side.

## Lake of the Isles Segment
Length: 2.9 miles
Come for a leisurely ride to view some of the grand historic homes in Minneapolis - when this neighborhood was built in the 1880s no house could cost less then $3000.

## Cedar Lake Segment
Length: 1.68 miles
The west side of Cedar Lake has a paved bicycle path that will connect you with Wirth Park. However, if you have a mountain bike it is possible to navigate around the entire lake using dirt trails on the north side (yield to pedestrians!) and maintenance trails along railroad tracks on the east side. This is an excellent lake for swimming and picnicing.

## Theodore Wirth Parkway Segment
Length: 6 miles
This is the largest park in the Minneapolis park system with an internal six-mile loop for both pedestrians and bicyclists. This park includes an 18 hole golf course, a par 3 course, concessions at the Wirth Chalet (at the golf course), picnic facilities, swimming beach, the Eloise Butler Wildflower Garden and Bird Sanctuary, the J.D. Rivers Children's Garden and a remnant of a Quaking Tamarack Bog, all of which are surrounded by natural woodlands, ponds and creeks. Be on the look out for wildlife, especially deer. During the winter, Wirth park offers cross-country and downhill skiing and tubing.

## Victory Memorial Parkway Segment
Length: 2.84 miles
Victory Memorial Drive is a three mile parkway lined with trees and plaques memorializing the servicemen from Hennepin County who died in World War 1. Stop and visit the Grand Army Circle and War Shrine located along the Drive.

## Central River Front Segment
Length: 1.4 miles
This is a relatively new development along the Central Riverfront that includes promenades, walking and biking trails, woodlands, picnic

areas and easy access to the waters edge–bring your fishing gear! This is also the annual site of fireworks for the 4th of July. Two regional amenities not to be missed while visiting the Mississippi Mile are Nicollet Island and Boom Island, both located on the east side of the river. You gain access by taking either the Hennepin Avenue or Plymouth Avenue bridges across the river.

## James J. Hill Stone Arch Bridge

This hundred year old railroad bridge was recently reopened as a bicycle and pedestrian facility–no cars allowed! This bridge offers a spectacular view of St. Anthony Falls (the only falls on the entire length of the Mississippi River) and connects Central River Front Trail to the on-road route near the University. Watch barges and pleasure boats work their way through the locks (Lock and Dam #1) on the west side of the bridge.

## Nicollet Island Segment

Length: less than 1 mile

Nicollet Island has picnic tables, a large pavilion (with restrooms), an amphitheater and sweeping views of the Mississippi River and Downtown Minneapolis. Nicollet Island is also home to De La Salle–the only high school in the continental United States located on an island. If you have time, bike through the residential north end of the island to enjoy a couple dozen beautifully restored historic homes. Take the crushed limestone trail along the northeastern edge of the island to connect with Boom Island. Boom Island is the largest riverfront park in Minneapolis and includes a boat launch, docks, promenades, picnic areas, open fields, restrooms, drinking fountains and a playground. Also a great place to fly a kite. Have time for a riverboat cruise? Then jump aboard the Anson Northrup for a different view of the river.

## Great River Road Segment (a.k.a. West River Road)

Length: 5.4 miles

This scenic connection between the Central Riverfront and Minnehaha park beautiful during autumn. This section of river includes scenic overlooks, picnic tables and scattered benches for resting. The east side of the river includes extensive sand dunes for sun-bathing and some trails for mountain biking (but yield to pedestrians!). [A bike loop can also be made along the river; start at Minnehaha Park, cross the Ford Parkway Bridge to the east side of the river; follow the bike path up the river a few miles to the Franklin Avenue bridge, cross it and rejoin the path on the west side to get back down to Minnehaha Park].

## Minnehaha Park Segment

Length: .5 miles

The crowning jewel of the Minneapolis park system includes the stunning Minnehaha Falls, extensive picnic facilities, hiking trails to the Mississippi River, a large refectory, gift shop, playgrounds, several historic statues and the Princess Depot. You may also wish to explore the Stevens House, the first frame dwelling erected west of the Mississippi.

Also near the park is the newly relocated Longfellow House Interpretive Center, a project of the City of Minneapolis and the Minneapolis Park and Recreation. It is located between Hiawatha Ave. and Minnehaha Ave. just south of Minnehaha Parkway.

Minnehaha State Park has become the focus of a critical link for bicycle trails between the cities of St. Paul, Minneapolis, Bloomington, Richfield, Mendota Heights, Ft. Snelling and several government agencies. Although funds have not yet been made available to enable the Longfellow House to reach its full potential, the strategic location at the intersection of pedestrian and bicycle pathways will permit it to serve as an ideal environmental/information/interpretive center when the city and park boards elect to fund it.

The restoration of the House is a rare example of a cooperative effort between intergovernmental agencies and private citizens to effect the preservation and reuse of a historic landmark. Upon final completion of the connecting bikeways, Minnehaha State Park will link the Minneapolis and St. Paul Grand Rounds, as well as the suburban Snelling bike trails. The Mendota Bridge and the Ford Parkway Bridge will also connect to the Longfellow House.

### Minnehaha Parkway Segment
Length: 5 miles (from Minnehaha Park to Lake Harriet)
This winding scenic trail takes you along the wooded area of Minnehaha Creek. In the springtime be on the lookout for large stands of daffodils planted by volunteers from People for Parks, a non- profit organization.

### Lake Nokomis Segment
Length: 2.7 miles
This regional amenity includes a swimming beach, large playing fields, concession, walking and biking paths and a community center with a gym. During the Aquatennial (held in late July) Lake Nokomis plays host to an annual triathalon and the "famous" milk-carton boat races.

### *FOR MORE INFORMATION:*
For more information, call 612-661-4800 or write:
The Minneapolis Park and Recreation Board
200 Grain Exchange Building
400 S. 4th Street
Minneapolis, Minnesota 55415-1400

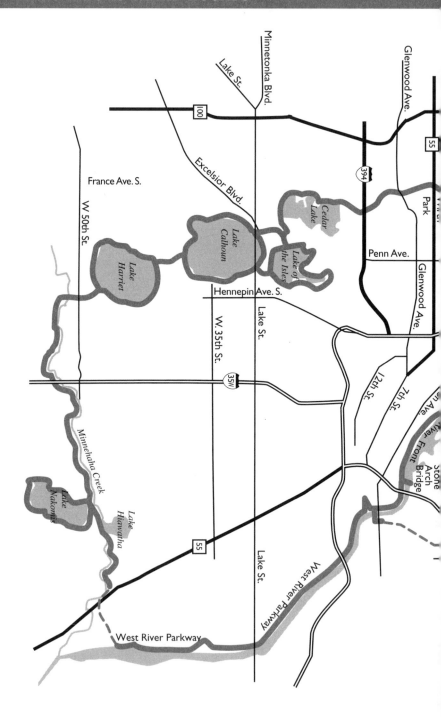

**WHERE:** Shakopee-Chaska
**LENGTH:** 6.5 miles completed to date
**SURFACE:** Paved
**TRAIL USE:** 🚴 🚶 ⛺ ➡️ 🎿 🐎

**Trailhead East:** At Murphy's Landing, two miles east of Shakopee. However, flooding washed out part of the trail, so the best bet is to start in Shakopee. The best access is in the Veteran's Memorial Park, between Shakopee and Murphy's Landing, where you will find parking, water and restrooms.

**Mid Access:** At Huber Park, near downtown Shakopee and the City Hall, a short block north of the stop light, where Highway 169 turns north to cross the river. Free parking, food and restrooms are available here.

**Trailhead West:** At Courthouse Lake, near the Carver County Courthouse, in southeast Chaska. Parking is available here.

Some 24,000 acres of parks, wildlife areas and trails comprise the Minnesota Valley system within which a 86-mile bicycle and hiking trail will be located. The area is managed for multiple purposes and trail construction is progressing as funds become available. The majority of the trail is presently open to only horseback, some mountain biking and winter recreation. Recent floods have further delayed improvements.

The trail will traverse both public and private lands and connect five counties and numerous communities along the south side of the Minnesota River. As yet, the only paved trail portion extends from Murphy's Landing 2 miles east of Shakopee to the Chaska city limits.

Because of its short distance, this is a popular hiking and in-line skating trail, in addition to bicycling. It is quite level and sheltered, following an old rail bed. The DNR has provided benches at intervals and a highlight is crossing the Minnesota River on the original railroad swing bridge

### FOR MORE INFORMATION:

Minnesota Valley State Park
19825 Park Boulevard
Jordan, MN 55352
612-492-6400

Minnesota River Valley
Headquarters
County Road 57
Jordan, MN 55352
612-492-6400

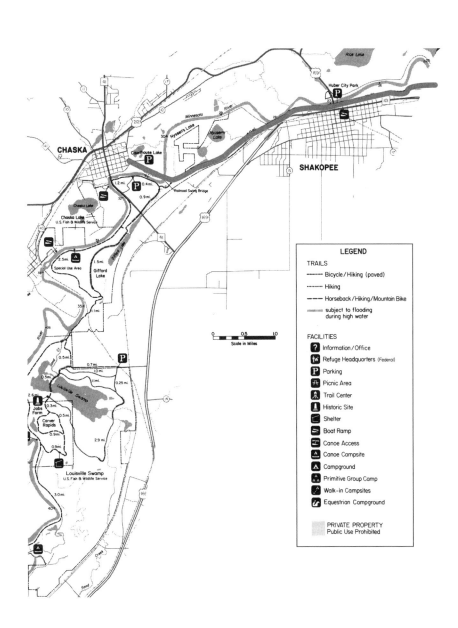

**LEGEND**

TRALS

----- Bicycle / Hiking (paved)

·········· Hiking

– – – Horseback / Hiking / Mountain Bike

▨▨▨▨ subject to flooding
during high water

FACILITIES

❓ Information / Office

🏠 Refuge Headquarters (Federal)

🅿 Parking

🔆 Picnic Area

🔒 Trail Center

🚹 Historic Site

📷 Shelter

🛥 Boat Ramp

🛶 Canoe Access

🛶 Canoe Campsite

⛺ Campground

⛺ Primitive Group Camp

⛺ Walk-in Campsites

🐴 Equestrian Campground

PRIVATE PROPERTY
Public Use Prohibited

**WHERE:** Coon Rapids Dam to Camden Bridge
**LENGTH:** 10.5 miles
**SURFACE:** Paved, 8' wide
**TRAIL USE:**

**Access:** Available from numerous streets in Coon Rapids, Fridley and Columbia Heights. However, we highly recommend one of the Anoka County Parks. Islands of Peace, Manomin, Riverfront Regional Park, Riverview Heights, and the Coon Rapids Dam all have ample parking and restrooms.

Scenic river overlooks, the Springbrook Nature Center and Banfill-Locke Arts Center in Manomin Park are some of the attractions along this trail, which makes for an excellent short ride, or a part of a longer ride, through the metro biking system. Although some of it is along city streets, it is well-marked and most is off-road.

Anoka County has a terrific park system and has connected many of them with a super bike route. This trail parallels the river, and passes through or near the Coon Rapids Dam Park, Riverview Heights Park, Manomin, Islands of Peace and Riverfront Regional Park, in addition to connecting with the Minneapolis Trail System.

From 86th Avenue, a striped and signed bike lane continues south on Mississippi Blvd. until reaching Broad Avenue. From Broad Avenue South, the trail alternates from off-road to marked roadside until crossing East River Road where it becomes off-road all the way to St. Anthony Parkway.

## *FOR MORE INFORMATION:*

Anoka County Parks
550 N.W. Bunker Lake Blvd.
Anoka, MN 55304
612-757-3920

*Phil and Marlys Mickelson near Lake Kohlmeier*

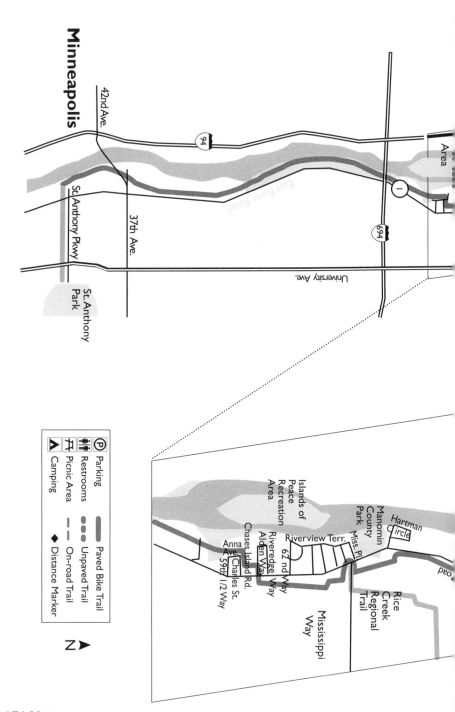

Minneapolis

42nd Ave.

94

St. Anthony Pkwy.

37th Ave.

St. Anthony
Park

East River Road

University Ave.

1

694

Area

**Legend**

Ⓟ Parking
🚻 Restrooms
🇫 Picnic Area
▲ Camping

━━━ Paved Bike Trail
••• Unpaved Trail
— — On-road Trail
◆ Distance Marker

N ▶

Islands of
Peace
Recreation
Area

Manomin
County
Park

Hartman
Circle

Chases Island Rd.

Riveredge
Way

Alden Way

62nd Way

Riverview Terr.

Miss. Pl.

Anna
Ave.

59th
1/2 Way

Charles St.

Mississippi
Way

Rice
Creek
Regional
Trail

Rice Creek Road

**WHERE:** Brooklyn Park
**LENGTH:** 7.2 miles (also connects to 9.3 mile Elm Creek Trail)
**SURFACE:** Paved
**TRAIL USE:** 🚲 🚶 🛏 ➜ ⛷ 🐎

**Access:** Available at several locations along the trail.

This is a very flat trail connecting the Elm Creek Park Reserve and the Coon Rapids Dam Regional Park.

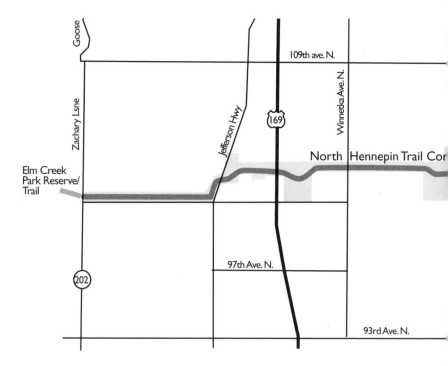

## FOR MORE INFORMATION:

Hennepin Parks
12615 County Rd. 9
Plymouth, MN 55441
612-559-9000

This is one of the few trails in the metro area with a parallel trail open to horses, snowmobiles and cross-country skiing. Crossing the Mississippi River at Coon Rapids will connect you with the Anoka County Trail system.

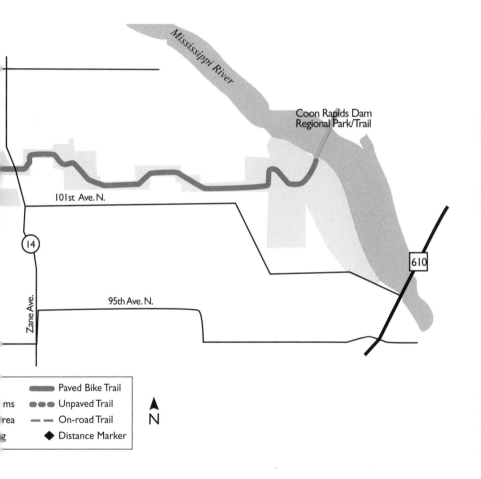

**WHERE:** St. Paul
**LENGTH:** 4.5 miles
**SURFACE:** Paved, 10' wide
**TRAIL USE:** 🚲 🚶 📷 ⛷

**Trailhead North:** At the intersection of Wheelock Parkway, Johnson Parkway and East Shore Drive, at the south end of Lake Phalen, where there is a small parking lot.

**Trailhead South:** At east 7th St. in Swede Hallow Park.

This is a new trail that takes advantage of the Phalen Creek waterway, which will provide safe hiking, biking and skating in a heavily populated area near downtown St. Paul. There is on-road parking only along most of this trail.

## FOR MORE INFORMATION:

Phalen Center
1000 E. Wheelock Parkway
St. Paul, MN 55106
651-298-5721

St. Paul Parks & Recreation
300 City Hall Annex
St. Paul, MN 55102
651-266-6400

**WHERE:** Fridley
**LENGTH:** 4.25 miles
**SURFACE:** Paved, 8' wide
**TRAIL USE:**

**Access:** The best parking and facilities are located in the park south of 69th Avenue at the east end just inside the park at the south side of the Target Northern Distribution Center, near the Columbia Arena, east of University Avenue. There is also a trail branch which leads to the dead end of Monroe Street if you enter the park from the south.

This is an excellent short trail through a scenic area. Expect foot and in-line skate traffic throughout.

Connecting bikeways: The trail hooks up with the Trailhead West of the North Mississippi Trail at the junction of Mississippi Street and East River Road. This permits access off Stinson Blvd. At Stinson Boulevard (Ramsey County line), the trail follows the east side of road to the southeast corner of Rice Creek Park. It also connects with Ramsey County Trail system at 69th Avenue and Stinson.

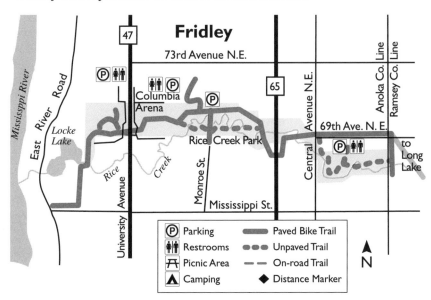

## FOR MORE INFORMATION:

Anoka County Parks
550 N.W. Bunker Lake Blvd.
Anoka, MN 55304
612-757-3920

**WHERE:** Hopkins to Victoria
**LENGTH:** 15.5 miles
**SURFACE:** Hard packed limestone, 10' wide
**TRAIL USE:**

**Trailhead East:** At the west side of 8th Avenue North, just north of Main Street in downtown Hopkins. There is parking available at 8th & Excelsior Avenue (County Road 3) on the south side.

Note: To connect to the LRT South Corridor, follow 8th Street south 1½ blocks to Excelsior Avenue, and the parking lot on the south side. The trail is adjacent to the parking lot.

**Mid Access:** Because the trail traverses from Hopkins to Minnetonka, Deephaven, Greenwood, Excelsior and Shorewood and terminates in Victoria, there are numerous access points.

**Trailhead West:** At Victoria there is a kiosk at Victoria Drive and Steigor Lake Lane, one block north of Highway 5. The trail actually continues west one-quarter mile but there is no parking available.

With the exception of the half mile of its eastern end in Hopkins, it is surprisingly secluded, with infrequent crossings of streets and roads. This rail bed (as well as the South Corridor route) was acquired by the Hennepin County Regional Railroad Authority and is leased to and managed by the Hennepin County Parks. As is the case with the South Corridor, it may someday become a light rail transportation route instead of a bike trail.

Just west of Hopkins, the trail parallels Minnetonka Boulevard for a time but, as we headed west from the Minnetonka Civic Center, we traveled wooded and remote wetlands most of the way to Excelsior. In Deephaven the trail crosses Carsons Bay with a great view of Lake Minnetonka and the marina. Further west, the trail again affords views of the lake and also crosses St. Albans Bay. At that point, it is necessary to leave the trail and follow well-marked streets through Excelsior to a resumption of the rail bed where you will again ride through secluded and interesting country into Victoria.

### FOR MORE INFORMATION:

Hennepin County Parks
French Regional Park
12615 County Road
Plymouth, MN 55441
612-559-9000

Trail Hotline 559-6778

Twin West Chamber of Commerce
10550 Wayzata, Blvd.
Minnetonka, MN 55305
612-540-0234

Shakopee Chamber of Commerce
1801 E. Highway 101
Shakopee, MN 55379
612-445-1660

**WHERE:** Hopkins to Chaska
**LENGTH:** 11.5 miles
**SURFACE:** Hard packed limestone, 10' wide
**TRAIL USE:**

**Trailhead East:** At the south side of Excelsior Avenue at 8th Street in Hopkins, the Park and Ride lot.

Note: If you wish to connect to the North Corridor LRT, cross Excelsior on 8th Street at the west end of the parking lot. Go 1½ blocks north on 8th and you will see the North Corridor access on the west side of 8th Street.

**Mid Access:** There are numerous streets and roads that intersect the trail, but for parking availability and easy access we recommend: Evandale Park, Miller Park and Reiley Lake Park.

**Trailhead West:** The kiosk on Bluff Creek Road, which is about one block west of the Highway 169, 101 and 212 intersection north of Shakopee, where Highway 169 crosses the Minnesota River. Here, you will find parking and portable restrooms. The trail actually extends one-half mile west of the kiosk but there is no access.

The trail surface had a few rough spots, due to recent heavy rains, but was generally excellent. Street crossings are relatively few. Some of the crossings, however, we found less than obvious and/or not well-marked. While riding from the south into Hopkins we totally missed the following crossings: The crossing at Highway 5: Go east via the sidewalk to first stoplight then back on sidewalk to trail. The crossing at Valley View Road: Cross where tail drops down to road level (no stop light), then left a short distance, you will see sign pointing to regain LRT. The crossing at W. 62nd (Crosstown): The trail goes under the bridge and at the top crosses back over the bridge (signs).

The day we rode, we encountered two Rangers patrolling the trail, one by bicycle, and very few trail users. Wherever high grades occur, 6' steel link fences have been installed. Side trips to the swimming beach at Lake Reilly and Shady Oak are easy and we predict you will find this a most enjoyable outing.

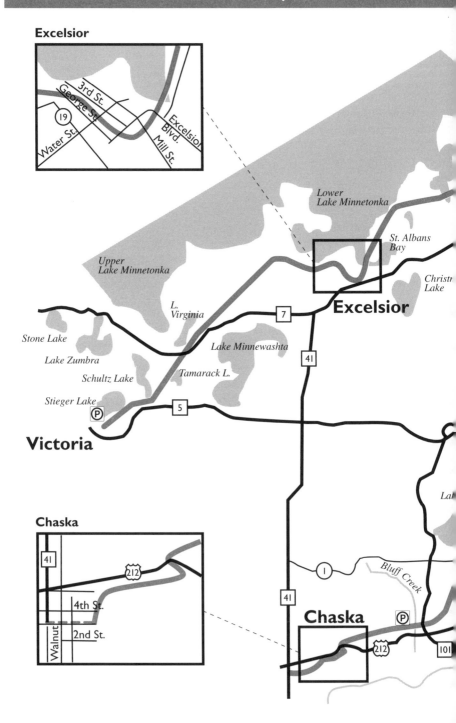

**Excelsior**

3rd St.

George St.

19

Water St.

Excelsior Blvd.

Mill St.

Lower Lake Minnetonka

St. Albans Bay

Christ Lake

Upper Lake Minnetonka

**Excelsior**

L. Virginia

7

Stone Lake

Lake Minnewashta

41

Lake Zumbra

Schultz Lake

Tamarack L.

Stieger Lake

5

**Victoria**

**Chaska**

41

212

4th St.

Walnut

2nd St.

La

Bluff Creek

1

41

**Chaska**

P

212

101

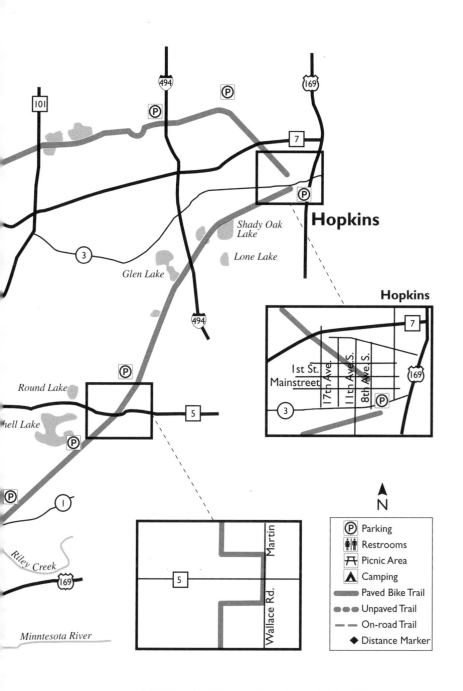

**Hopkins**

**Hopkins**

Shady Oak Lake

Lone Lake

Glen Lake

Round Lake

hell Lake

Riley Creek

Minntesota River

1st St.

Mainstreet

17th Ave.

11th Ave. S.

8th Ave. S.

N

| | Parking |
|---|---|
| | Restrooms |
| | Picnic Area |
| | Camping |
| | Paved Bike Trail |
| | Unpaved Trail |
| | On-road Trail |
| ◆ | Distance Marker |

Martin

Wallace Rd.

Administered by Minnesota Department of Natural Resources

**WHERE:** St. Paul
**LENGTH:** 28 miles
**SURFACE:** Paved off-road and some paved road shoulder
**TRAIL USE:**

**Access:** At any location throughout the circle route around the city.

For points of interest, convenience, parking and facilities, we especially recommend the following:

| | |
|---|---|
| Hidden Falls Park | Crosby Farm Park |
| Grand Rounds North | Phalen Park, beach and restaurants |
| Como Park | Indian Mounds Park |
| (pool, zoo, snacks) | (best view in town) |

Lower Landing Park at the foot of Jackson Street

Although not entirely off-road, the St. Paul Grand Rounds provides an excellent tour of urban St. Paul and the Mississippi River valley. The Grand Round Loop connects almost all of St. Paul's major parks and parkways (e.g. Mounds Park, Johnson Parkway, Phalen Park, Wheelock Parkway, Como Park, Midway Parkway, Pelham Boulevard and Mississippi River Boulevard, Hidden Falls Park, Crosby Farm Park) and bikeways along the Mississippi. It was first envisioned over a century ago by park system planners and nationally prominent landscape architect Horace W.S. Cleveland.

It will also provide connections to the Munger-Gateway State Trail, the Minneapolis Grand Rounds bikeways, the Stone Arch Bridge and downtown Minneapolis, in addition to the Minneapolis trails bordering the banks of the Mississippi. Other connections will further extend the potential ride to Ft. Snelling and perhaps all the way to Le Sueur.

**West Section**
The Mississippi River East Bank Trail extends from Emerald Ave. and Mississippi River Boulevard on the north (where it connects to the East River Road segment of the Grand Rounds Parkway System in Mpls.) to south of the Ford Plant and then splits at Hidden Falls Park.

**South Section**
A branch goes through Hidden Falls and Crosby Farm Park (see page 145). Another branch follows Mississippi River Boulevard past Fort Snelling and the Mendota Bridge to become a separate paved trail paralleling Shepherd Road from I-35E to Randolph Avenue. It also has a paved walking trail, except on bridges, but the trail evaporates at Chestnut Street near downtown St. Paul, necessitating about one mile of on-street riding until a new and wider segment can be picked up going east from Jackson Street, in Lower Landing Park. This new sec-

tion of the Mississippi River Trail is 10' wide paved with a separate walking trail. It extends east nearly 2 miles before ending at the bridge over Childs Road. There is excellent parking at Lower Landing Park. East of Childs and Fish Hatchery Roads the trail bridges over Warner Road to connect to Indian Mounds Park and Johnson Parkway. Another branch goes south to connect with Battle Creek Trail (see page 142) and a route on and along Point Douglas Road.

## East Section

The eastern loop of the Grand Rounds follows Johnson Parkway as a marked, on-street route 2½ miles north from Burns Avenue at the north edge of Indian Mounds Park to Wheelock Parkway and the Lake Phalen Park Trail system (see page 156).

## North Section

The north loop of the Grand Rounds follows Wheelock Parkway as a well-marked, on-street route west 4 miles to Lake Como and the Como Park System. (See page 143) From Lake Como, the Grand Rounds continues west as an on-street lane on Como Avenue to the intersection with Raymond Street. An alternative route follows Midway Parkway and Commonwealth Avenue through the State Fair Grounds (closed during the State Fair) and the St. Paul campus of the U of M.

Dropping south on Raymond to Myrtle, the on-street trail jogs two blocks over to Pelham where it again heads south to connect with the Mississippi River Trail and the west section.

Now included in the St. Paul trail system is a paved route south of the river from Warner Road and past the Yacht Club on Harriet Island. From the Yacht Club a paved road shoulder follows Water Street all the way to Lilydale Park where it connects to the Big River Trail (see page 135). A word of caution: the road shoulder is 3' wide or less in spots, but road traffic is usually light. Via the Mendota Bridge, this will also provide another link with the Minneapolis Trails. Also new and connecting to the Grand Rounds is an off-road paved trail following the transit way from the St. Paul campus of the University of Minnesota and ending at Energy Park near the Minneapolis campus. This trail will eventually connect to the Minneapolis trail system via the Stone Arch Bridge. There is now a downhill, signed, on street trail from there to Stone Arch Bridge.

### FOR MORE INFORMATION:

St. Paul Parks & Recreation
300 City Hall Annex
St. Paul, MN 55102
651-266-6400

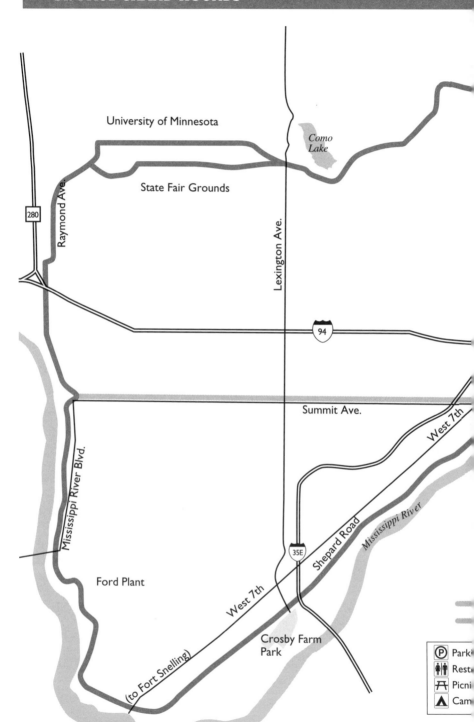

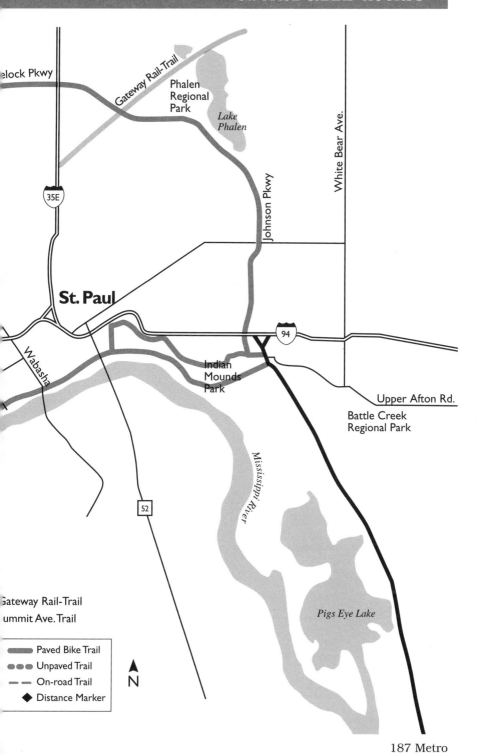

elock Pkwy

Gateway Rail-Trail

Phalen Regional Park

*Lake Phalen*

White Bear Ave.

Johnson Pkwy

35E

**St. Paul**

Wabasha

94

Indian Mounds Park

Upper Afton Rd.

Battle Creek Regional Park

*Mississippi River*

52

*Pigs Eye Lake*

Gateway Rail-Trail
ummit Ave. Trail

Paved Bike Trail
Unpaved Trail
On-road Trail
Distance Marker

▲
N

**WHERE:** St. Paul
**LENGTH:** 5 miles
**SURFACE:** Signed and striped on-street bike lanes
**TRAIL USE:** 🚴 🚶 🛼 🎿

**Trailhead West:** Connects to the Mississippi River Trail at Mississippi River Road.

**Trailhead East:** At John Ireland Boulevard and I-94, near the State Capitol and the St. Paul Cathedral. The planned extension of the Munger Gateway State Trail and further extension of this one will eventually connect the two.

This is a well-marked bicycle lane along and through a scenic and historic section of central St. Paul. Summit Avenue is on the longest and best preserved grand Victorian Boulevard in the United States; the entire length of Summit is on the National Register of Historic

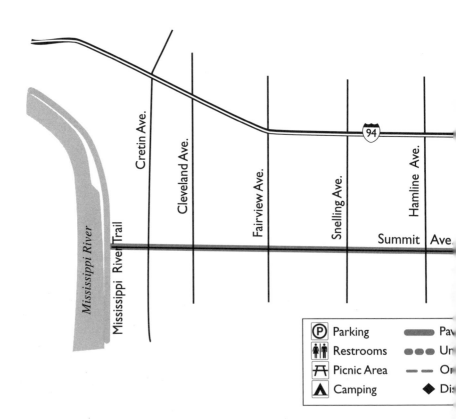

Places. There are numerous good restaurants along Grand Avenue, one block south of Summit, especially near Victoria Street and Macalester College.

For a shorter version (14 miles) of the Grand Rounds, take this, Mississippi River Boulevard, and Shepherd Road past the high bridge to Chestnut, then Chestnut Street north to Summit Avenue.

---

### *FOR MORE INFORMATION:*

St. Paul Parks & Recreation
300 City Hall Annex
St. Paul, MN 55102
651-266-6400

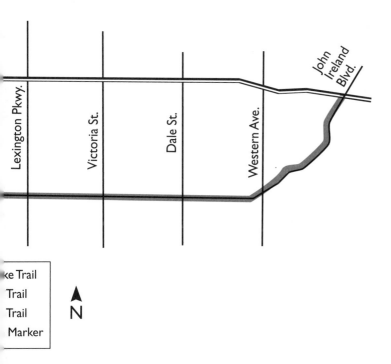

**WHERE:** Marine on St. Croix
**LENGTH:** 2 miles
**SURFACE:** Paved
**TRAIL USE:** 🚴 🚶 ⛺ ✈ ⛷ 🐎

**Access:** State Highway 95 two miles north of Marine-on-St. Croix.

This park was named after William O'Brien, a logger who bought surrounding river front land after it was logged. Now a haven for wildlife and variety of vegetation, this park also offers fine swimming on Lake Alice, canoe and boat rental (for both lake and river). The Interpretive Center and trail center is open year round, offering lots of programs and activities. Bulletin boards post those schedules.

---

### Bike Shorts

Minnesota has more miles of paved rail to trail bikeways than any other state.

The Willard Munger Trail from Hinckley, MN to Duluth, MN is currently the longest paved rail-trail in the nation.

The Heartland Trail in Minnesota, dating to 1975, is the oldest paved rail-trail in the nation.

---

### *FOR MORE INFORMATION:*

William O'Brien State Park
16821 O'Brien Trail North
Marine on St. Croix, MN 55042
651-433-0500

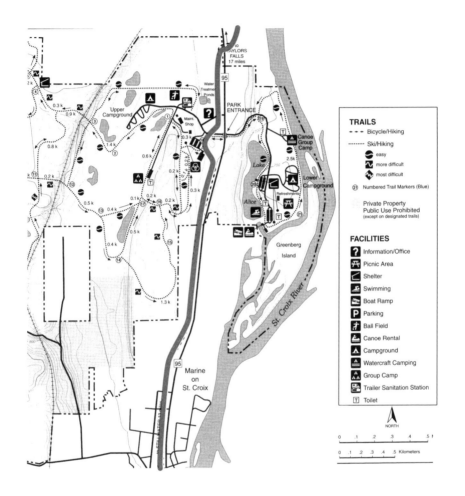

**TRAILS**

- - - Bicycle/Hiking

· · · · · · Ski/Hiking

~ easy

~ more difficult

~ most difficult

(21) Numbered Trail Markers (Blue)

Private Property
Public Use Prohibited
(except on designated trails)

**FACILITIES**

? Information/Office

🔆 Picnic Area

⛺ Shelter

🏊 Swimming

🚤 Boat Ramp

P Parking

⚾ Ball Field

🛶 Canoe Rental

▲ Campground

⛺ Watercraft Camping

▲▲ Group Camp

🚽 Trailer Sanitation Station

T Toilet

NORTH

0   .1   .2   .3   .4   .5 Miles

0   .1   .2   .3   .4   .5 Kilometers

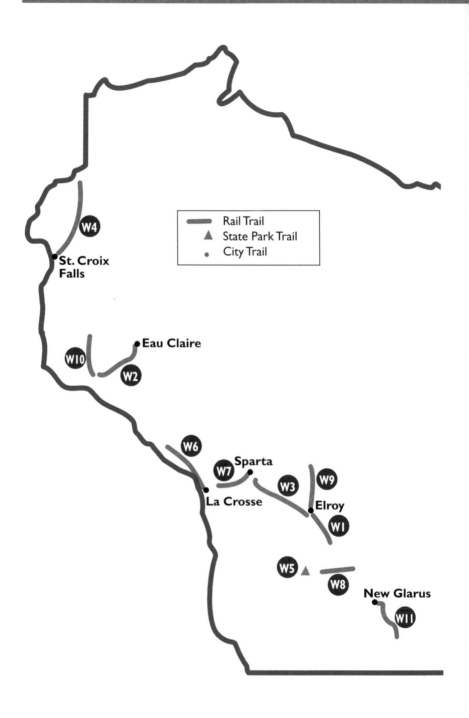

Rail Trail
State Park Trail
City Trail

St. Croix Falls

Eau Claire

W4

W10

W2

W6

W7

Sparta

W3

W9

La Crosse

Elroy

W1

W5

W8

New Glarus

W11

# Western Wisconsin

**\* Numbers refer to large map on page 11 and opposite page**

## WISCONSIN INFORMATION

Although paved trails in Wisconsin are relatively few, the increasing popularity of in-line skating, as well as hiking, is bringing more demand for asphalt. More paving such as was done on the Chippewa River and Omaha Trails can be expected in the future.

The Wisconsin DNR Bureau of Parks and Recreation has a continuing program of expansion and improvement of its off-road biking systems. Wisconsin currently maintains over 470 miles of improved rail bed trails.

Most of the rail bed trails are surfaced with crushed limestone and intersect with numerous small communities providing frequent access, rest and refreshment stops. Quite recently, individual counties have constructed trails with the assistance of and under a memorandum of agreement with the Wisconsin State DNR. In those cases, the county supervises and maintains the trail and may or may not charge the same fee as the state. Current user fees for county trails are indicated with each county trail in this book as is the county headquarters phone number should you desire additional information.

Wisconsin trail hours are 6:00 AM to 11:00 PM. Although most remain surfaced with screened, crushed limestone, there is expanded use of hard surfacing on some of the newest trails.

Wisconsin State Trails require trail user fees. Daily passes are $3.00 per day or a season pass is available for $10.00. Passes are available at all trail headquarters, from rangers you may encounter along the trail, from businesses near the trail in non-headquarter communities (inquire locally), or from DNR at the following address:

> Wisconsin Department of Natural Resources
> Park Division, P.O. Box 7921
> Madison, WI 53707
> 608-266-2181

The Wisconsin Department of Tourism has available a comprehensive publication, "Wisconsin Biking Guide" which is free. It includes 15 off-road trails, 14 on-road bike tours and 14 mountain bike trails with maps of most of them. Write or call:

> The Department of Tourism
> 201 W. Washington, P.O. Box 7976
> Madison, WI 53707-7976
> 608-266-2161, 800-372-2737.

Individual trail maps are now available from the Bicycle Federation of Wisconsin at the following address. Maps are grouped by each quarter of the state and you will receive all maps within a specified area for $3.95 plus $2.00 handling, or all four maps for $12.95 plus $5.00 handling. Write or call:

Bicycle Federation of Wisconsin
104 King Street, Madison, WI 53707
608-251-4456, 800-362-4537.

## Bike Shorts

Biking is second only to walking as the most popular outdoor sport activity in Minnesota. Bikeways have been the most requested recreational facility since 1983.

The most certain way to ride regularly is to develop a group of interested friends.

**WHERE:** Elroy to Reedsburg
**LENGTH:** 22 miles
**SURFACE:** Crushed limestone
**TRAIL USE:**

**Trailhead North:** At the Commons in Elroy.

**Mid Access:** At Union Center, Wonewoc and LaValle.

**Trailhead South:** At Reedsburg.

A scenic ride paralleling the Baraboo River, this trail includes ten river crossings as well as a number of feeder streams. The Baraboo is popular with canoeists and you may also encounter horseback riders because a horse trail runs alongside the 400 between Wonewoc and LaValle.

This trail gets its name from a very well-known passenger train of its day, the old Chicago Northwestern "400" from Chicago to the Twin Cities.

Three Wisconsin bike trails merge in Elroy where the city has recently developed a downtown park with connections to each trail. The Commons provide parking, restrooms, pay showers, lockers, picnic facilities and even a "tot lot." Restaurants, stores and the Elroy Area Historical Society are all nearby.

Note: There is a new country trail connecting Hillsboro and Highway 80 to the 400 Trail at Union Center. It is paved and 3 ½ miles long. (Wildcat State Park is near Hillsboro)

*FOR MORE INFORMATION:*

The Depot
240 Railroad Street, P.O. Box 142
Reedsburg, WI 53959-0142
608-524-2850
800-844-3507

Elroy Commons
303 Railroad Street
Elroy WI 53959-0142
608-462-2453
888-606-2453

## Bike Shorts

Padded cycling gloves reduce tiring and numbness of hands and wrists.

If it clicks, scrapes, squeaks or rattles, your bike needs fixing.

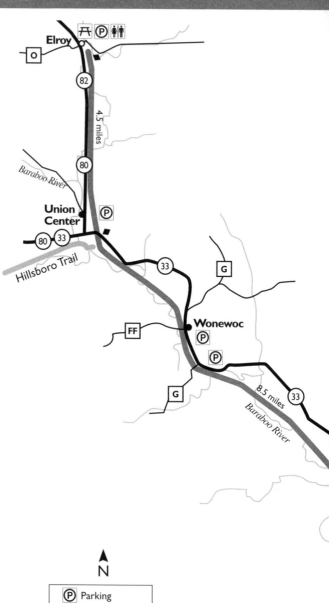

Redstone
Lake

Twin Creek

Hay Creek

58

V

9 miles

33

58

La Valle

Reedsburg

# CHIPPEWA RIVER STATE PARK

**WHERE:** Eau Claire to Red Cedar State Park Trail
**LENGTH:** 20 miles
**SURFACE:** Asphalt from Eau Claire to Caryville. Asphalt emulsion Caryville to the west trailhead.

**TRAIL USE:** 🚲 🚶 🏕️ ➡️ ⛷️

**Trailhead East:** The trail begins in downtown Eau Claire, at First Avenue along the Chippewa River. Parking and trail access are also available at the University campus, located at 1st and Water Street.

**Mid Access:** At Meridean and Caryville. Also at the Highway 85 wayside park, located 8 miles from Eau Claire. The wayside park offers parking, restrooms and water.

**Trailhead West:** As yet, the Wisconsin DNR has not been successful in obtaining public access to the point where the Chippewa Trail connects with the Red Cedar State Park Trail. The best bet for now is to take County Road Y east at Dunnville, and ride the Red Cedar State Park Trail for the short distance south across the bridge.

This is one of the few Wisconsin State Trails with a surface other than crushed limestone. It is an easy trail, though somewhat open, so wind may be a factor.

See map pages 202.

***FOR MORE INFORMATION:***

Western Division DNR
1300 W. Clairmont Avenue,
P.O. Box 4001
Eau Claire, Wi 54701-6127
715-839-1607

Eau Claire Area Convention
and Visitors Bureau
800-344-3866

**WHERE:** Menomonie to Chippewa River State Trail
**LENGTH:** 14.5 miles
**SURFACE:** Crushed limestone
**TRAIL USE:**

**Trailhead North:** On Highway 29 in west Menomonie at Riverside Park. Take the second exit west of the Highway 29 bridge to the renovated depot.

**Mid Access:** At Irvington on Highway D (mile 2.7), Downsville on Highway 25 (mile 7.5), and Dunnville on Highway Y (mile 12.5).

**Trailhead South:** The trail ends after crossing the Chippewa River on an 800-foot trestle at the junction with the Chippewa River State Trail, off of County Road M.

As with most Wisconsin trails, the Red Cedar is surfaced with well-maintained crushed limestone. On this trail, you will pass through woodlands, prairies and unique rock formations. For most of its distance, the trail overlooks the Red Cedar River, which is also popular with canoeists. Several picnic tables have been provided in scenic spots where you can rest and relax.

Just after crossing the Chippewa River, you connect with the western end of the new Chippewa River Trail. We found the wide and sandy shores of the Chippewa to be an excellent picnic spot. This trail also offers riders the opportunity to ride an 800-foot trestle, perhaps the longest of any bike trail, and enjoy a spectacular view in the process.

Since its total length is only 14½ miles, this is a very manageable two-way ride, no matter where you start. Give yourself some extra time for this ride since there are so many interesting things to see and do along the way. In the area you will find the Downsville Cooperative Creamery, which was founded in 1904 and currently houses a restaurant, lounge and four room inn, in addition to the showroom and shop where Dunn County Pottery is designed and created.

See map pages 202.

### FOR MORE INFORMATION:

Red Cedar State Park Trail
921 Brickyard Road
Menomonie, WI 54751-9100
715-232-1242

Greater Menomonie Area
Chamber of Commerce
700 Wolske Bay Road, Suite 200
Menomonie, WI 54751
715-235-9087, 800-283-1862

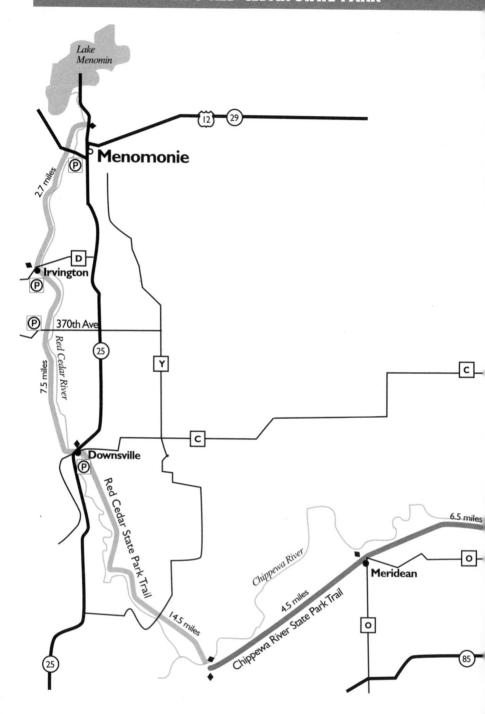

*Lake Menomin*

12 29

**Menomonie**

P

2.7 miles

D

**Irvington**

P

P 370th Ave

7.5 miles

*Red Cedar River*

25

Y

C

C

**Downsville**

P

Red Cedar State Park Trail

*Chippewa River*

6.5 miles

O

**Meridean**

4.5 miles

14.5 miles

Chippewa River State Park Trail

O

25

85

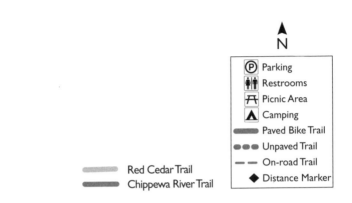

N

| | |
|---|---|
| Ⓟ | Parking |
| ♀♂ | Restrooms |
| 🪑 | Picnic Area |
| ▲ | Camping |
| ▬▬ | Paved Bike Trail |
| ●●● | Unpaved Trail |
| – – | On-road Trail |
| ◆ | Distance Marker |

▬▬ Red Cedar Trail
▬▬ Chippewa River Trail

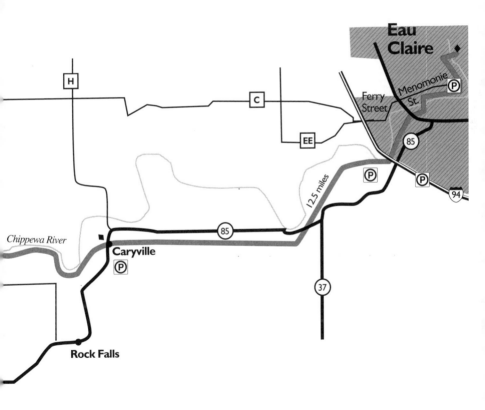

**WHERE:** Sparta to Elroy
**LENGTH:** 32 miles
**SURFACE:** Crushed limestone
**TRAIL USE:**

**Trailhead West:** At exit I-90 at Highway 27, Sparta. Start at the newly renovated depot at South Water and Milwaukee (also the east terminus of the LaCrosse State Trail, page 216). Follow the well-marked city streets south out of town to the actual trailhead on the left of the road. There is also parking here.

**Mid Access:** At Norwalk on Highway 71 and County Road T (trail mile 11.9), at Wilton on Highway 71 and County Road M (trail mile 17.3), and at Kendall on Highway 71 and County Road W (trail mile 26.4). The trail headquarters is located at Kendall, 5.7 miles from the east trail access.

**Trailhead East:** At the west edge of Elroy, just north of Highway 71. Three Wisconsin bike trails merge in Elroy, where the city has recently developed a downtown park with connections to each trail. The Commons provide parking, restrooms, pay showers, lockers, picnic facilities and even a "tot lot." Restaurants, stores and the Elroy Area Historical Society are nearby.

The Elroy-Sparta Trail traverses the Hidden Valley country of Wisconsin providing spectacular scenery as well as great bird watching and possible wildlife sightings. (The entire trail is a wildlife refuge.) The area is heavily-wooded, providing shelter from sun and wind. The woods also make this an extremely popular ride during the fall color season.

The rugged and scenic attraction of the area probably tells you this trail is not the level or gradually-inclined roadbed of the prairie or river bottom. In fact, there are few level stretches, with long, rather steep (for a rail bed) inclines. The long upgrades are matched by equally long downgrades that give you the chance to rest up. This trail does, however, require more physical conditioning and stamina than most 32 mile rides.

There are three upgrades, each leading to tunnel cuts through solid rock. Those tunnels make the trail unique. Tunnel 3, at mile 12.4 from the west end, is seven-tenths of a mile long. Tunnel 2, at mile19.5, is three-tenths of a mile long and tunnel 1, at mile 25.3, is one-quarter of a mile long. For tunnel 3, special equipment not taken along on most bike trips is highly recommended. A three-quarter mile tunnel is long and dark and you will need a flashlight. You may need an extra wrap as tunnels can be both cold and damp. You will need to walk your bike at least through tunnel 3, so it will take awhile. The spirit of adventure provided by the tunnels really adds something special to this trip.

In the valleys between each tunnel (as well as at each end) are interesting small towns that truly welcome bikers and provide food, refreshments and restrooms. Of special interest is the refurbished depot at Kendall which has been designated a national historic landmark. It also serves as the trail headquarters and a railroad museum.

For the casual or weekend biker, a one-way trip is a full day ride. This necessitates staying overnight or dropping a car at one end. Should your party want to drop a car, Highway 71 parallels the trail all the way. If you have only one vehicle, this is one of the few trails that provides a driver service. Take two sets of keys with you and pick up a driver at the Kendall headquarters. The driver will drop you at your starting point and return your car to Kendall. There is a nominal fee and reservations are recommended.

The foresight of responsible individuals and the State of Wisconsin has provided us with a truly exceptional bike trail in an unusually scenic area. It has been maintained and in use since 1965 and has become well known nationally among biking enthusiasts.

While you're in the area, you might want to check out Kendall's annual Labor Day weekend celebration which features a parade, dance and plenty of barbecued chicken and sweet corn. In Wilton, the Lions Club serves pancake breakfasts in the municipal park Sunday mornings from June to September. Finally, you'll find that Sparta has a 34-acre lake.

## FOR MORE INFORMATION:

Bike Trail Headquarters
Kendall Depot
P.O. Box 297
Kendall WI 54638-0297
608-463-7109

Elroy Commons
303 Railroad Street
Elroy, WI 53929
608-462-2453,888-606-2453

Sparta Chamber of Commerce
111 Milwaukee Street
Sparta, WI 54656
608-269-4123, 800-354-2453

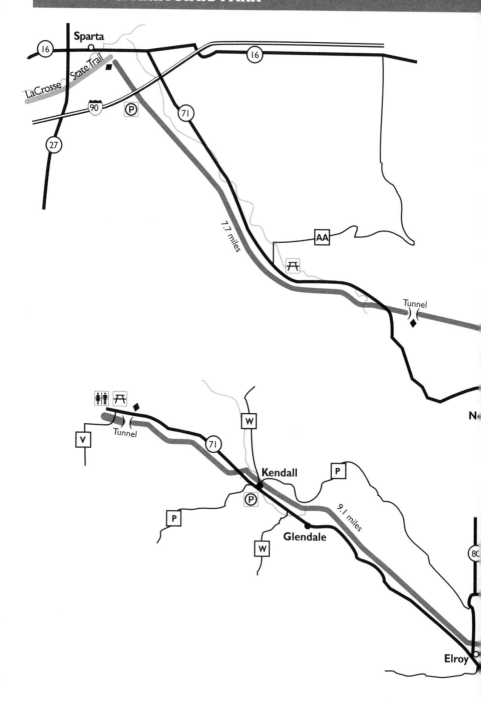

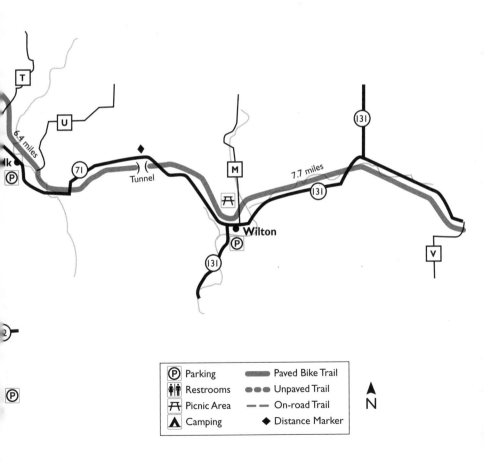

T

U

6.4 miles

71

Tunnel

◆ Distance Marker

M

7.7 miles

131

131

Wilton

131

V

131

2

Parking

Restrooms

Picnic Area

Camping

Paved Bike Trail

Unpaved Trail

On-road Trail

◆ Distance Marker

N

**WHERE:** Danbury to St. Croix Falls
**LENGTH:** 47 miles
**SURFACE:** 10' wide crushed limestone
**TRAIL USE:**

**Trailhead South:** The Polk County Information Center at the Junction of Highways 8 and Highway 35. You will find parking and restrooms there.

**Mid Access:** The trail passes through Centura, Milltown, Luck, Frederic, Lewis, Siren and Webster. In our opinion, Frederic, Siren and Webster offer the best parking near the trail.

**Trailhead North:** At Danbury. The trail terminates at Highway 77, on the west edge of town. There is parking here. The ATV, snowmobile and horse trail continues north from Highway 77. The St. Croix State Park, on the Minnesota side of the river, is just a short ride west on Highway 77 from the trail access.

The existence of this trail is the result of unique cooperation between Burnett and Polk Counties, and the Wisconsin Department of Natural Resources. The DNR secured the railroad right-of-way and the counties undertook the construction, maintenance and administration. This trail is jointly administered by Polk and Burnett Counties Park & Forestry Department.

The old rail bed and right-of-way crosses into Minnesota a short distance north of Danbury via a high trestle over the scenic St. Croix River. This unimproved 51-mile segment extends all the way from Danbury to Superior with Minnesota responsible for completing about two-thirds of that and Douglas County, Wisconsin responsible for one-third. Although improvement of this segment is not planned for the near future, the Gandy Dancer will eventually extend a wonderful 98 miles. (Note: A "Gandy Dancer" is the historical nickname for railtrack-laying workmen.)

In Polk County the trail crosses three bridges and utilizes two tunnels under highways. It also features scenic cuts through rock outcroppings, woods and open farmlands that border the trail. In Frederic, the Depot is being refurbished as a museum.

In Burnett County the trail passes through woods, wetlands and farmlands. En route you will cross five bridges and have a good chance of spotting wildlife.

## Bike Shorts

A large plastic bag takes little space and makes good emergency rain cover.

Always carry your own water bottle. For a cool drink, fill your water bottle the night before and freeze overnight.

### FOR MORE INFORMATION:

Burnett County Forest and
  Parks Department
7410 County Highway K
Box 106
Siren, WI 54872
715-349-2157

Burnett County Web Site
www.mwd.com/burnett/

Burnett Department of Tourism
  7410 County Road K, Box 112
Siren, WI 54872
800-788-3164

Polk County Information Center
710 Highway 35 South
St. Croix Falls, WI 54024
800-222-7655, 715-483-1410

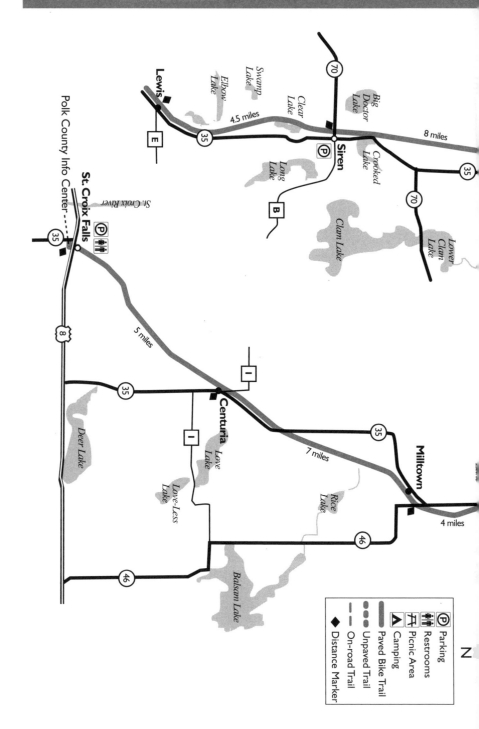

Legend:
- P Parking
- Restrooms
- Picnic Area
- Camping
- Paved Bike Trail
- Unpaved Trail
- On-road Trail
- ◆ Distance Marker

N

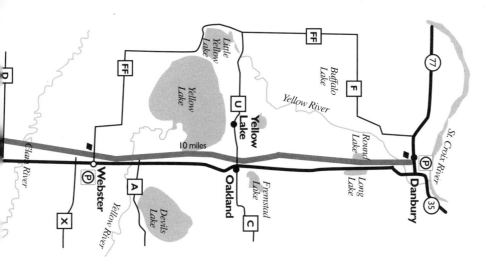

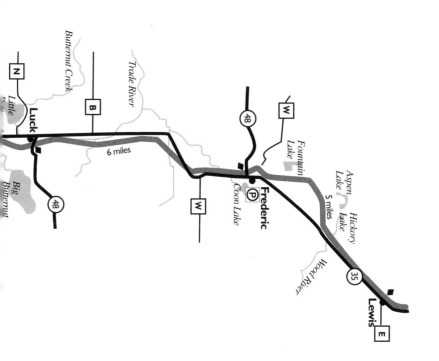

**WHERE:** South of Marshland to Onalaska
**LENGTH:** 24 miles
**SURFACE:** Crushed limestone
**TRAIL USE:**

**Trailhead North:** South of Marshland, Wisconsin, on Highway 35, there is a parking lot that serves as the trailhead. There are no restrooms here. The trail does not follow the rail bed until you leave the wildlife refuge. About one mile down the trail you have the option of taking the loop through the refuge. There is no fee to use the trail through the refuge.

**Mid Access:** There are parking lots at Perrot State Park, Lytles and Midway. Near the city of Trempealeau, on Highway 35, there is a large parking lot with portable restrooms.

**Trailhead South:** The separate rail bed trail ends near downtown Onalaska where it continues about four blocks on city streets. The streets are well-marked and bring you to the actual trailhead at the Center for Commerce and Tourism, a four-year-old brick building with restrooms and ample paved parking at 800 Oak Forest Road. From the same building, there is a paved connection to the parking lot and west trailhead of the LaCrosse River State Trail (see page 216) just south of Highway 16. At substantial expense, the state recently built a bridge over some active railroad tracks to permit a safe, off-road connection between these two trails.

For a close-up look at waterfowl, wildlife, river bottoms and bluffs, this Wisconsin trail is an excellent choice. Generally sheltered and shaded, it crosses two national refuges and 18 bridges, including one that is 1226 feet long.

Because of the scenery, a side trip through Perrot State Park, and watching a tow lock through Lock & Dam #6, we found this trail took a bit more time than its 24 miles would indicate. Although riding both ways in one day is not unreasonable, you may prefer a more leisurely trip for these same reasons. We found overnighting in Trempealeau suited our schedule, riding south 14 miles and then back one afternoon, and then north the 10 miles and back the next morning.

## Bike Shorts

Rail beds provide opportunity for bike trails that require little surface preparation and little tree removal. They also often provide access to scenic vistas not otherwise available.

Footwear is important in biking. Choose shoes with a fairly rigid sole.

### FOR MORE INFORMATION:

Perrot State Park
P.O. Box 407
Trempealeau, WI 54661
608-534-6409

Onalaska Tourism
800 Oak Forest Drive
Onalaska, WI 54650
800-873-1901

Trempealeau Chamber of Commerce
P.O. Box 212
Trempealeau, WI 54661-0212
608-534-6780

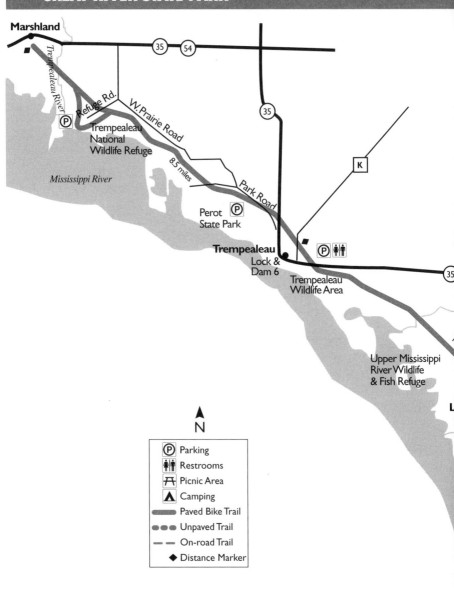

**Marshland**

35 54

35

Refuge Rd.

W. Prairie Road

*Trempealeau River*

Trempealeau
National
Wildlife Refuge

8.5 miles

Park Road

*Mississippi River*

Perot
State Park

K

**Trempealeau**
Lock &
Dam 6

Trempealeau
Wildlife Area

35

Upper Mississippi
River Wildlife
& Fish Refuge

L

N

| | |
|---|---|
| Ⓟ | Parking |
| 🚻 | Restrooms |
| ⊼ | Picnic Area |
| ▲ | Camping |
| ▬ | Paved Bike Trail |
| ●●● | Unpaved Trail |
| – – | On-road Trail |
| ◆ | Distance Marker |

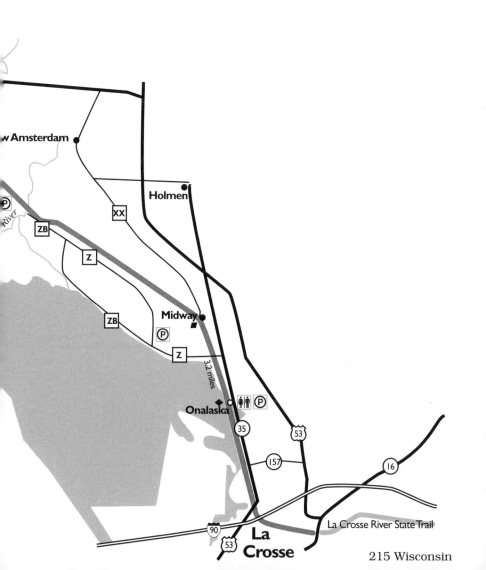

**WHERE:** LaCrosse to Sparta
**LENGTH:** 21.5 miles
**SURFACE:** Crushed limestone
**TRAIL USE:**

**Trailhead West:** Exit Highway 16 East at the stop lights at the Highway B intersection in north LaCrosse. Go approximately one-quarter mile on Highway B to the Medary parking lot, on the left.

**Mid Access:** Highway 108 south of West Salem. Bangor and at intersecting county roads.

**Trailhead East:** On the south edge of Sparta. Follow the street signs to the renovated depot at the intersection of South Water and Milwaukee in Sparta. You will find ample parking and facilities in Sparta.

This is one of the newer rail-trails in western Wisconsin and connects the Great River and Elroy-Sparta trails. Its roadbed and bridges are in excellent condition and the length provides a challenging two-way ride or an easy one-way day trip.

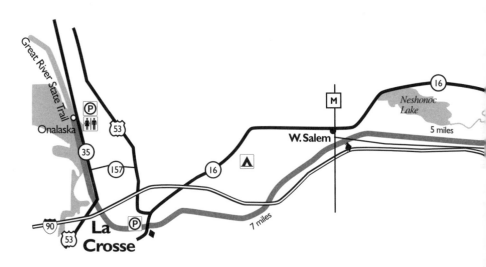

Much of its 21½ miles parallels the LaCrosse River and provides a variety of scenery including farmlands, hardwood forests and wetlands. It also parallels I-90 for much of the distance between north LaCrosse and Sparta. Unfortunately, there are some points where this detracts somewhat from the serenity of the ride. The connection to the Great River State Trail takes you north on County Road B, under Highway 16 and over a recently completed bridge spanning active rail tracks. From the bridge, the paved connection continues to the Onalaska Center for Commerce and Tourism at 800 Oak Forest Road. The latter is the southern trailhead of the Great River State Trail (see page 212).

## FOR MORE INFORMATION:

LaCrosse River State Trail
P.O. Box 99
Ontario, WI 54651
608-337-4775

Onalaska Tourism
800 Oak Forest Drive
Onalaska, WI 54650
800-873-1901
Open weekends May-October

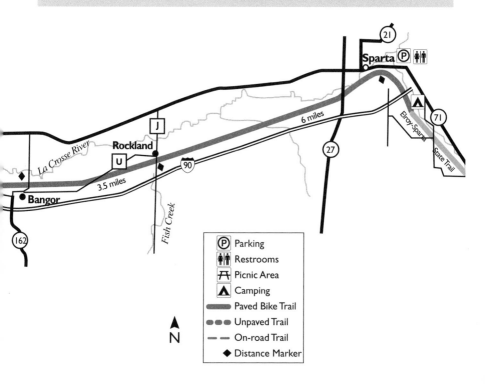

| | |
|---|---|
| Ⓟ | Parking |
| 🕴🕴 | Restrooms |
| 🔾 | Picnic Area |
| ▲ | Camping |
| ▬▬ | Paved Bike Trail |
| ●●● | Unpaved Trail |
| – – | On-road Trail |
| ◆ | Distance Marker |

**WHERE:** Verona to Dodgeville
**LENGTH:** 39.6 miles
**SURFACE:** Crushed limestone
**TRAIL USE:**

**Trailhead East:** The trail actually begins one mile east of Verona but this location offers no facilities. The trail runs through Verona where you will find everything you need including parking, restrooms, bike repair and trail passes.

**Mid Access:** At Riley at County Road J, Klevenville on County Road P, Barneveld at County Road T, Ridgeway at County Road H, and Mt. Horeb, the trail's midpoint, which has a trailside parking lot, but no restrooms, located 1½ blocks south of County Road PD on either 1st or 2nd Street. Also, the Blue Mounds State Park has parking and restrooms.

**Trailhead West:** At Dodgeville, just east of Highway 23 and County Road YZ. At the 2½ mile connection to Governor Dodge State Park you will find parking but no restrooms. Parking and facilities are available in other sections of the park (see page 219 for park trails)

Military Ridge Trail follows a route originally traveled by buffalo and Indians. Part of this route was converted to a Highway by General Zachary Taylor and subsequently the path became a rail bed.

This is an historic and scenic ride with a maximum grade of one-half percent. Along the route you will encounter 48 planked bridges. We found the Mt. Horeb to Verona portion to be the most scenic although it is also the more difficult of the two halves. The grade rises almost all the way west from Verona back to Mt. Horeb.

This is one of the oldest trails in Wisconsin and has shelters and picnic tables at scattered locations, but most facilities are provided by the communities and businesses along the trail.

In the area you will find the Blue Mounds, Governor Dodge State Parks, Little Norway and the trolls of Mt. Horeb. Finally, Madison is only a short distance from Verona.

---

### FOR MORE INFORMATION:

Military Ridge State Park Trail
P.O. Box 98
Blue Mounds, WI 53517
608-935-5119

Dodgeville Chamber of Commerce
Dodgeville, WI 53533
608-935-5993

**GOLD MINE TRAIL:** 2.5 miles
**MEADOW VALLEY:** 6.8 miles
**MILL CREEK:** 3.3 miles
**USER FEES:** The park honors State Trail passes
**TRAIL USE:**

Located just north of Dodgeville, this park is one of the largest in Wisconsin. With over 12 miles of paved trail and a paved connection to the well-known Military Ridge State Park Trail, this park should be considered as a scenic addition to any Military Ridge trip. These are not rail-trails so expect some hills. The park trails connect with Military Ridge Trail just east of County Road Z in north Dodgeville (see page 218).

The Gold Mine loop is a short meandering trail through scenic woods and meadows, with a minimum of hills. The Meadow Valley loop begins at the Cox Hollow Lake beach. It has some steep hills, but is very scenic. Also beginning at the Cox Hollow Lake beach, the Mill Creek trail connects with the Military Ridge Trail to the south.

On any of the park trails you will encounter hikers, and some portions also allow horse riders. As a result, caution is advised.

---

### *FOR MORE INFORMATION:*

Governor Dodge State Park
4175 State Highway 23 North
Dodgeville, WI 53533
608-935-2315

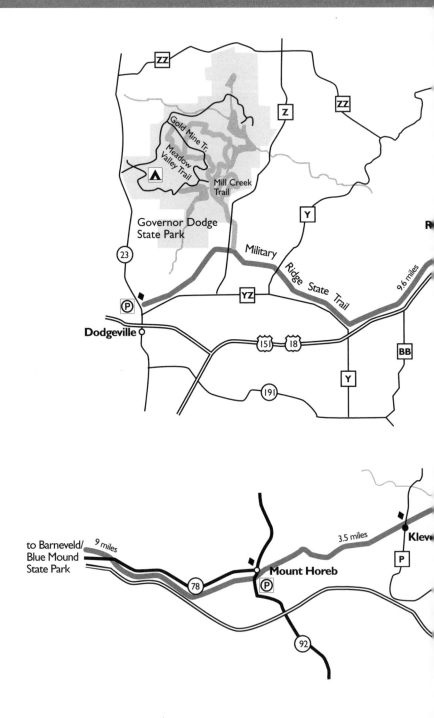

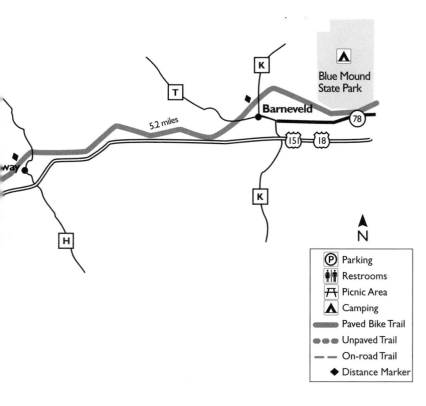

Blue Mound
State Park

K

T

5.2 miles

Barneveld

78

151    18

way

K

H

N

Parking
Restrooms
Picnic Area
Camping
Paved Bike Trail
Unpaved Trail
On-road Trail
Distance Marker

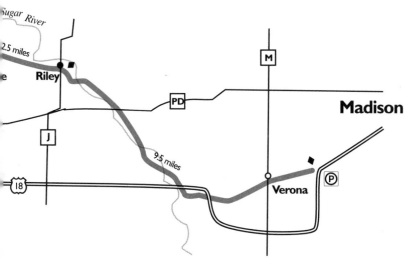

Sugar River

2.5 miles

Riley

M

PD

Madison

J

9.5 miles

18

Verona    P

**LENGTH:** 12.5 miles
**SURFACE:** Paved
**TRAIL FEE:** $1.00 per day or $5.00 for the season.
**TRAIL USE:**

**Trailhead South:** At the Commons in downtown Elroy. You will find full facilities here including pay showers, lockers, restrooms and a picnic area.

**Mid Access:** At Hustler, on County Road A. The city park has parking and restrooms.

**Trailhead North:** At Camp Douglas, one-half mile south of I-94 at exit 55.

This trail is county owned and constructed. It is one of the newer trails in the state. Connecting to the Sparta-Elroy and the 400 Trail at Elroy, it is a beautiful ride by itself, or as an addition to either of the DNR Trails out of Elroy.

This trail traverses wooded, rolling and open vistas. It also includes 12 bridges, an overpass over Highway 80, and a tunnel over 600 feet long. At the tunnel, you will find a small park and picnic area with restrooms.

### *FOR MORE INFORMATION:*

Juneau County Forestry and Parks
250 Oak Street
Mauston, WI 53948
608-847-9389

Elroy Commons
303 Railroad Street
Elroy, WI 53929
888-606-2453
608-462-2453

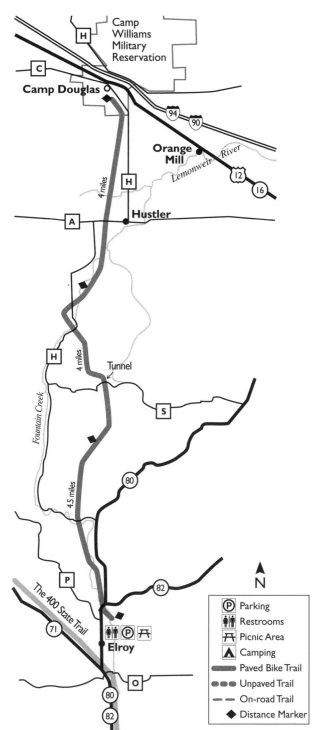

Camp Williams Military Reservation

Camp Douglas

94 90

Orange Mill

Lemonweir River

12

16

4 miles

Hustler

A

H

H

C

Fountain Creek

4 miles

Tunnel

S

80

4.5 miles

P

82

The 400 State Trail

71

Elroy

O

80

82

N

| | |
|---|---|
| Ⓟ | Parking |
| 🚻 | Restrooms |
| ⛱ | Picnic Area |
| ▲ | Camping |
| ▬ | Paved Bike Trail |
| ●●● | Unpaved Trail |
| – – | On-road Trail |
| ◆ | Distance Marker |

223 Wisconsin

**WHERE:** New Glarus to Brodhead
**LENGTH:** 22.6 miles
**SURFACE:** Crushed limestone
**TRAIL USE:**

**Trailhead North:** The trail headquarters is located in the old depot at Highway 69 and 39 in New Glarus. You will find parking and restrooms there. You may get your permit here, rent a bike and inquire about shuttle service.

**Mid Access:** At Monticello on Highway 69 you will find trailside restrooms, water and parking.

**Trailhead South:** At Brodhead on Highway 11. There are trailside restrooms, water and parking located at west 3rd Avenue and Exchange Street.

An interesting and scenic ride through the heart of the Swiss Community of southwest Wisconsin, referred to as the Uplands, this trail runs through beautiful countryside from New Glarus to Brodhead, Wisconsin. The trail is flat and smooth and offers appropriate biking for the entire family.

The trail is packed with limestone screening for comfortable travel through picturesque rolling hills, verdant meadows and state wildlife refuges. The trestle bridges over rushing streams have planked floors and safety railings.

New Glarus is home to some of the Midwest's finest specialty foods. The butcher shops feature kalberwurst, landjaeger and homemade bratwurst. The baker makes Swiss bratzeli cookies, fastnacht juechli and a holiday stollen that is shipped all over the nation during the holidays. The trail's surrounding countryside is where some of the finest cheeses in the United States are made. There are many great restaurants here, too. Wisconsin's #1 tourist attraction, Frank Lloyd Wright's House on the Rock at Spring Green, is nearby as well as historical Mineral Point.

---

### *FOR MORE INFORMATION:*

Sugar River State Trail
PO Box 781
New Glarus, WI 53574
608-527-2334

## Bike Shorts

Allow for less efficient braking in wet weather or after riding through a puddle. Water on your rims and brakes can double required stopping distance.

Time your ride to avoid rush hour traffic. Midday on weekdays and weekends are the safest times to ride.

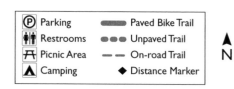

| | | | |
|---|---|---|---|
| ℗ Parking | | ▬▬ Paved Bike Trail | |
| 🚹🚺 Restrooms | | ●●● Unpaved Trail | |
| 🎪 Picnic Area | | – – On-road Trail | |
| ▲ Camping | | ◆ Distance Marker | |

N

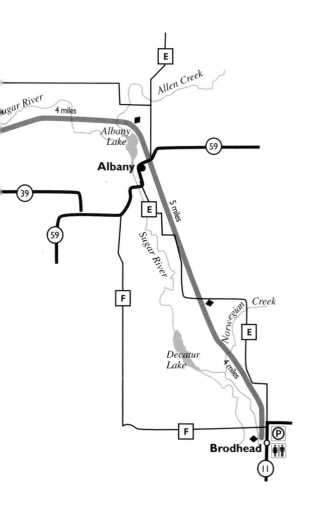

Minnesota has a continuing rail-to-trail acquisition and development program which will improve existing trail systems and take advantage of some of the hundreds of miles of abandoned rail bed remaining in the state. Present plans include the following, which will be incorporated in future editions of this book as they are added to the trail system.

## Paul Bunyan
The continuation from Hackensack to connect to the Heartland Trail just south of Walker. 218-828-2693

## Glacial Lakes
Extending the trail from New London to Richmond — 25 miles. Presently crushed rock from New London to Hawick, undeveloped to Richmond. 320-354-4940

## Taconite Trail
The challenge to completing the trail north and east out of Grand Rapids is terrain, not right-of-way. 218-327-4408

## Gateway Trail
The 1998 Legislature appropriated funds, planning to extend the Gateway from Pine Point Park to O'Brien State Park on the St. Croix River. 651-772-7935

## Mill Towns Trail
A paved recreational trail in the works that would link the Cannon Valley Trail (Cannon Falls to Red Wing) and the Sakatah Singing Hills Trail (Faribault to Mankato). Call Northfield Chamber of Commerce for updated information. 507-645-5604

## Harmony–Preston Valley
A six mile paved spur from Preston trail headquarters west to Forestville State Park is planned to be added as soon as funds become available. 507-467-2552

## Blufflands Trail System
An extensive trail system is in the planning stages for Fillmore and Houston counties. Already named are the Blazing Star, Prairie Wildflower and Shooting Star. 507-467-2552, 800-428-2030

### Agassiz Trail
A Joint Powers Board is developing an old rail bed through Polk, Clay and Norman Counties running from Ulen north. Thirty-five miles are now open to mountain biking. Eventually this will be a 72-mile trail. 218-584-5169

### Soo Line Trail
Extensions 20 miles west from Onamia to Genola and east from Isle to Munger and Duluth is in this trail's future. 320-983-2561

### Willard Munger
Much remains to be done to span the gap between the north end of the Gateway Segment and the Hinckley-to-Duluth segments. 218-485-5410

### Gandy Dancer
A 90-mile trail originating and ending in Wisconsin, the Minnesota segment enters at Danbury and parallels the state line to exit just south of Superior. See Wisconsin Rail-Trail section page 192. 715-349-2157

### Minnesota Valley National Wildlife Refuge and Recreation Trail
Most of the right-of-way has been secured to permit an 86-mile multi-use trail from Fort Snelling State Park to Le Sueur. 612-492-6400

## BICYCLE HEADGEAR

*Reprinted from July 1989 "Mayo Clinic Health Letter" with permission of Mayo Foundation, for Medical Education and Research, Rochester, Minnesota.*

### Bicycle Helmets
Protective headgear can be a lifesaver.

It's as easy as falling off a bicycle.

The adage has been around for decades. Unfortunately, it makes light of the potential for tragedy if you should take a serious fall while riding a bicycle.

With an increasing number of people riding bicycles on our streets and highways, the risk of injury, in particular head injury, continues to rise. Each year, nearly 50,000 bicyclists suffer serious head injuries. According to the most recent statistics, head injuries are the leading cause of death in the approximately 1-300 bicycle-related fatalities that occur annually. To a large extent, these head injuries are preventable.

Wearing a helmet can make a difference. Until recently, advocates of the use of protective headgear for cyclists found their stance lacked scientific support. But wearing protective headgear clearly makes a difference. Recent evidence confirms that a helmet can reduce your risk of serious head and brain injury by almost 90 percent should you be involved in a bicycle accident.

### What to look for in a bicycle helmet

We endorse these guidelines for bicycle helmets recommended by the American Academy of Pediatrics:

The helmet should meet the voluntary testing standards of one of these two groups: American National Standards Institute (ANSI) OR Snell Memorial Foundation. Look for a sticker on the inside of the helmet.

1) Select the right size. Find one that fits comfortably and doesn't pinch.

2) Buy a helmet with a durable outer shell and a polystyrene liner. Be sure it allows adequate ventilation.

3) Use the adjustable foam pads to ensure a proper fit at the front, back and sides.

4) Adjust the strap for a snug fit. The helmet should cover the top of your forehead and not rock side to side or back and forth with the chain strap in place.

5) Replace your helmet if it is involved in an accident.

## EQUIPMENT

The proper equipment for your intended level of biking is an important factor in your safety and enjoyment. All bike shops offer a wide selection of equipment, accessories and clothing and can best advise you on your specific needs.

### Basic Equipment

1) Most bicycle shops have "fit kits" to precisely advise on proper fit for your body. A rule of thumb is to straddle the bike with feet flat on the floor and close together. There should be 2 to 3 inches clearance. Your bike shop professional will help you with this.

2) Touring seats and handlebars are more comfortable for casual biking. Racing handlebars put considerable pressure on wrists and hands in addition to the strain on your neck from riding with your hands so low. Touring seats are wider and generally carry more padding–something most people appreciate. You can buy seat pads filled with gel or made of soft and comfortable sheepskin.

3) The angle of the seat is critical. It should be level and the height set so the leg is nearly fully extended when the pedal is in the full down position.

### Accessories

Realizing there are a multitude of accessories available, we will confine our comments to a very few which we have found to be most beneficial to our biking safety and pleasure. Of course, the most important is a good helmet but we also suggest the following to increase your comfort and enjoyment.

1) Seat pads filled with gel provide multiple return on the investment in the form of added comfort.

2) Padded bike shorts reduce chafing, absorb moisture and provide additional padding.

3) A rear view mirror (either helmet or handle bar mounted) is primarily a safety accessory but it also saves neck strain.

4) Padded gloves help reduce discomfort of weight and tension on the hands when subject to long periods in the same position.

5) Frame-mounted water bottle should be translucent to keep track of supply.

**Special Equipment:**
It is not necessary for certain equipment to be carried by everyone, but it is desirable that someone in the group carry a tire pump, patching material and some basic tools.

For example:
Screwdriver
6" or 8" adjustable wrench
Pair of small pliers
Accurate tire pressure gauge

Everyone should carry at least one bike bag. How many, size and style depend on the type of ride and length of trip you intend to make.

We recommend a handle bar bag for clothing and personal items on every bike. One insulated rear wheel bag is adequate for every two people. This may require a rear carrier bracket. Use one or two reusable containers of frozen liquid to ensure cold drinks and preserve food.

If your bike trip is an overnight, you will require larger saddle bag storage for extra clothing. Panniers are available for either front or back wheels.

### Minnesota Bikeways Maps

We recommend the Explore Minnesota Bikeways maps published by the Minnesota Department of Transportation and the Wisconsin Division of Tourism (see Wisconsin information, page 194). The Minnesota Bikeways maps include DNR and county-maintained rail-trails and maps of trails and bike paths in towns and along highways suitable for extended biking and of particular interest to long distance runners. Roads are color coded for biking suitability and contain information regarding road analysis for bicycle usage, paved road shoulders, off-road bikeways, bike-pedestrian bridges, controlled access roads (bicycles prohibited), historical and cultural attractions, public parklands and facilities. Maps are not current.

| Map | Includes inset of cities with trails: |
|---|---|
| Northeast | Duluth, Cloquet, Virginia, Hibbing, International Falls, Brainerd, Grand Rapids |
| Northwest | Detroit Lakes, Fargo/Moorhead, Little Falls, Grand Forks/E. Grand Forks, Bemidji, Thief River Falls, Fergus Falls, Crookston |
| Southeast | Owatonna, Mankato/N. Mankato, Albert Lea, Faribault, Austin, Rochester, Northfield, St. Cloud/Sauk Rapids, Red Wing, Winona, Stillwater, Hastings |
| Southwest | Marshall, New Ulm, Hutchinson, Worthington, Fairmont, Alexandria, Willmar |
| Metro East | |
| Metro West | |

Each map is $3.00 except the metro maps which are $2.00. There is a $2.00 mailing charge per order and a 6.5% sales tax (for MN residents only). Prices are subject to change without notice. Mail map orders to:

Minnesota Department of Transportation
John Ireland Boulevard, Room B-20
St. Paul, MN 55155
(no phone orders accepted)

or

Minnesota Bookstore
117 University Avenue (Ford Building)
St. Paul, MN 55155
612-297-3000 or 1-800-657-3757
Phone orders accepted
Mastercard, Visa, Discover, American Express

### State Bicycle Advisory Board

Minnesota has a full-time bicycle coordinator and State Bicycle Advisory Board. For additional information, safety brochures, etc. Contact:

State Bicycle Coordinator
State Bicycle Advisory Board
440 Transportation Building
395 John Ireland Boulevard
St. Paul, MN 55155

### Minnesota DNR

Individual maps of the 18 bicycle trails, state parks with bicycle paths and mountain bike opportunities are available at no charge.

Contact:

Minnesota Department of Natural Resources
Outdoor Information Center
Box 40, 500 Lafayette Road
St. Paul, MN 55155
612-296- 6157
Within Minnesota, toll free 888-646-6367

### Minnesota Office of Tourism

The Minnesota Office of Tourism has developed free directories for accommodations that you may order by phone or mail. *Explore Minnesota Hotels, Explore Minnesota Motels, Explore Minnesota Resorts, Explore Minnesota Campgrounds, Explore Minnesota Bed and Breakfast and Historic Inns,* all available from:

Minnesota Office of Tourism
100 Metro Square
121 Seventh Place East
St. Paul, MN 55101
800-657-3700 Metro Area: 296-5029